Matt;
The grace of God
will keep you as you
walk in Victory!

Eric A. Lambert Jr.

D1384219

THE **CHRISTIAN** & THE **CULTURE** II

Walking in Victory

Bishop Eric A. Lambert, Jr.

outskirts
press

Outskirts Press, Inc.
http://www.outskirtspress.com

ISBN: 978-1-9772-4022-4

Library of Congress Control Number: 2021906396

PRINTED IN THE UNITED STATES OF AMERICA

Table of Contents

Introduction

When I began writing the series on *The Christian and the Culture*, I intended to make it a three-part series. The first volume was a general observation regarding the modern struggles the Christian face in this culture. I wanted to focus on the passage in Romans where the Apostle Paul teaches us that we should not be poured into the mold of the world. The teaching of Romans 12 gives the Christian a mandate for mental and spiritual change.

This second book of *The Christian and the Culture* gives the Christian a list of steps to apply to walk in the victory our Lord gives to all of His children. I discovered many Christians do not know who they are and what is available to them as believers in the Lord Jesus. If we are to maintain a life of victory, we must practice these disciplines regularly. When we walk with Him, we must resist becoming what we behold in this world every day.

This volume takes the believer on an exciting ride into the life of victory. I focus on living a life of perpetual success and applying the teachings given to us by the Lord to live above the trappings of this world. I have dedicated a segment of this book to the development of the fruit of the Spirit. This is one area where I believe we are deficient and, most times, disconnected from the Lord.

My prayer is for you to not only enjoy the writings but to take a moment and review your walk with God. I am sure you will find some insight into your Christian life and look for ways to improve your relationship with our Father.

Blessings to all.

Bishop Eric A. Lambert, Jr.
Pastor
Bethel Deliverance International Church

Dedication

I dedicate this book to the memory of my mother and my father. Their teachings helped me to be the man I am today. While I thought their training was harsh, I realize now they were only looking out for my well-being. The example of my father taught me how a man should conduct himself. He also taught me the meaning of family pride and sacrifice. My mother taught me things about the love of family. She said we must always look out for each other and protect our family.

I believe we must put these principles into practice as members of the family of God. So, with those teachings and principles in mind, I dedicate this book to everyone in my family who had a hand in helping to raise me. God bless all of you.

A SPECIAL MESSAGE FROM THE AUTHOR:
TO ALL WHO READ THIS BOOK

Your walk with Christ is the best gift the Lord has given us. I pray you enjoy this book and rejoice in your relationship with our Heavenly Father.

BLESSINGS!

Chapter

1

Living in This Present World

For the grace of God that brings salvation has appeared to all men, teaching us that, denying ungodliness and worldly lusts, we should live soberly, righteously, and godly in the present age, looking for the blessed hope and glorious appearing of our great God and Savior Jesus Christ, who gave Himself for us, that He might redeem us from every lawless deed and purify for Himself His own special people, zealous for good works.

Titus 2:11-14 (NKJV)

Titus, the youthful disciple of the Apostle Paul, faces a significant responsibility. The church at Corinth is struggling with worldliness and fleshly demonstrations of spirituality. Fornication is rampant, and the level of idolatry has increased. Paul's first letter to the Corinthians brought about a level of repentance, and the people walked as believers in Christ. Faithfulness was being restored.

Then Paul sends Titus to Corinth with the second letter of reconciliation, and the message is clear: "Come out from among them, and do not touch the unclean."

Titus takes this opportunity to instruct believers in the behaviors and practices that will make them better examples of Christ.

One of the most definitive statements by Titus instructs the believers to live soberly, godly, and righteously in this present world. We can only hope that his audience took those words to heart and changed their lives as a result. Paul writes, "For the grace of God that brings salvation has appeared to all men, teaching us that, denying ungodliness and worldly lusts, we should live soberly, righteously, and godly in the present age, looking for the blessed hope and glorious appearing of our great God and Savior Jesus Christ, who gave Himself for us, that He might redeem us from every lawless deed and purify for Himself His own special people, zealous for good works. (Titus 2:11-14 NKJV)

God's message through Titus remains alive and vibrant for Christians today. But how are we to live Christ-centered lives in a world that seems to be increasingly spinning out of control? There are many satanic traps placed in front of us. We often hear the voice of the ungodly culture whispering that we cannot live above sin. Therefore, we must accept the flaws of others and those of ourselves as part of the human experience.

But is that God's view? Absolutely not! He has called us to holy lives of righteousness amid this secular, hedonistic society. How do we live above sin and embrace the Kingdom principles of God's plan? Is it possible to escape the snares of the Evil One in this life? Can we rise above our fallen nature, be washed of our sins, and cling to God's purity? The writer of the letter to the Hebrews exhorts followers of Jesus to do just that: *"Pursue peace with all people, and holiness, without which no one will see the Lord..."* (Hebrews 12:14 NKJV)

One reason for this series is to give Christian readers a better understanding of the challenges we face in our society. Over many years, our sermons have spoken out against overt sins and ignored the little things that lead to bondage. For example, we often hear warnings against murder, fornication, and stealing. These are highly destructive and wide-ranging sins.

However, we hear little about gluttony, greed, pride, and theft. People usually accept these behavioral problems as typical human nature. However, they weaken the Christian just as effectively as the "BIG" sins. These are the sins that our culture accepts, and this careless and condoning attitude has led us to accept them in the church. But we must remember the warning that Jesus gave His followers:

"Do not think that I came to destroy the Law or the Prophets. I did not come to destroy but to fulfill. For assuredly, I say to you, till heaven and earth pass away, one jot or one tittle will by no means pass from the law

3

till all is fulfilled. Whoever therefore breaks one of the least of these commandments, and teaches men so, shall be called least in the kingdom of heaven; but whoever does and teaches them, he shall be called great in the kingdom of heaven. For I say to you, that unless your righteousness exceeds the righteousness of the scribes and Pharisees, you will by no means enter the kingdom of heaven."

(Matthew 5:17-20 NKJV)

Christians cannot afford to become complacent about their culture. We know that temptation is everywhere, and excuses will not be accepted. We must stand against the pull of the enemy and discipline ourselves for the Holy Spirit to use us for the Glory of God. God's laws and principles are clearly stated in the Old Testament and the New Testament. The Apostle Paul clarifies critical issues of his culture. We must be vigilant to understand God's expectations for us and to withstand the wiles of the devil.

Let us take a closer look at the so-called "lesser sins" of our era, sometimes referenced among the many evil behaviors as defined by the Apostles. We must first identify our enemies before we can hope to defeat them, so here are several of the most common sinful practices that Christians are called to avoid.

ENVY

Envy means to covet something – to want something that you do not have or desire something that belongs to someone else. Have your eyes ever gleamed when that new car commercial came on during a TV program break? Your vehicle might be running just fine, but now you suddenly think you need a newer, later-model car, you know, to keep up with the Joneses next door who bought one last week. Remember that God promises to meet all your needs if you trust Him: " *But seek first the kingdom of God and His righteousness, and all these things shall be added to you.* " (Matthew 6:33 NKJV)

What if you did not have any car to drive? What if you lose your job next month? God knows what is best for you. Leave your life in His hands and focus on doing the work He has given you. Christians who have the habit of collecting expensive possessions and always wanting what they do not have will show unbelievers that we are part of their culture and are rooted in this materialistic world, not citizens of the next spiritual world.

GLUTTONY

According to the National Institute of Diabetes and Digestive Diseases and Kidney Diseases, a National Health and Nutrition Examination Survey in 2013-14 found that more than 1 in 3 adults were overweight. More than 2 in 3 adults were considered to be overweight or obese (https://www.niddk.nih.gov/health-information/health-statistics/overweight-obesity#).

Taxing our bodies and jeopardizing our health by carrying around significant extra weight is not treating our bodies as temples of the Holy Spirit! Nor are overweight Christians setting a positive example for the world who watches to see how we are different – and better or worse – than they are. With numerous restaurants to patronize and supermarkets to shop, we have an endless selection of exotic foods from around the world and the homegrown varieties of produce and meat that we enjoy so much. But we must learn to say no!

A pastor of a large Midwest church noticed that he was getting addicted to butter pecan ice cream and eating it almost every day. Refusing to let his appetite control his behavior, he stopped buying the ice cream regularly and instead enjoys it now and then. *And put a knife to your throat if you are a man given to appetite.* (Proverbs 23:2 NKJV)

If we practice the same problematic sins which dominate our culture, how can we be salt and light to the unsaved? They will scoff and ignore our efforts to acquaint them with the Bible if we do not take care of ourselves. When we love this world too much and overindulge in its pleasures, we become like the unbelievers, dimming the light within us that beckons others to Christ.

LUST

Within a couple of generations, sex has gone from closet secrecy to mainstream marketing via product advertising, internet pornography, and clothing styles – especially those of women. While sex has a place of honor within marriage according to God's plan, it was never intended to be a recreational outlet for base-minded people with nothing better to do.

The old advertising slogan, *sex sells*, rages on in today's postmodern world. Look at almost any evening television series, many or most recent films, and performances and videos by leading musicians – all these media and more leave little to the imagination. Even secular outcries have gone out against certain Superbowl halftime shows that reveal an embarrassing amount of flesh and body parts.

Satan knows exactly how to inflame lust in just about everyone. It is up to Christians to keep our eyes on God and our hearts protected from sinful desires. If you are married, savor the love of your spouse – be "enraptured" with your loved one, as Solomon urges in Proverbs. Do not be tempted to chase another person and commit adultery or fornication. Lust leads to worldly problems like disease, unplanned pregnancies, and broken relationships, and it can separate us from God's grace if we fail to repent. Do not fall into the cultural trap of letting animal instincts ruin your relationship with God and those you love. *The righteousness of the upright will deliver them, but the unfaithful will be caught by their lust.* (Proverbs 11:6 NKJV)

Tame your lust and direct your affection to the person you married. If you are single, wait for God to bring His designated mate for you into your life.

Sloth

The Merriam-Webster Dictionary defines sloth as "a disinclination to action or labor" and/or "spiritual apathy and inactivity" (https://www.merriam-webster.com/dictionary/sloth). In our hectic world, it is easy to keep a relationship with God out of our daily priorities. We get too busy to read the Bible, go to church, or help others in need. But we are seldom too tired to watch television, play video games, surf the internet, or spend time with friends. Christians cannot become slothful in their relationship with God. *He who is slothful in his work is a brother to him who is a great destroyer.* (Proverbs 18:9 NKJV)

You probably know people who seem "disinclined" to hold a job. They might be hard to motivate to help around the house or even get up in the morning. We sometimes refer to these individuals as lazy. Yet, are some of us "lazy" in our attitude toward God?

At the time of this writing, the US. unemployment rate is soaring – due mainly to the COVID-19 pandemic that has forced people into quarantine and businesses to close. Unfortunately, many of these companies will never reopen. The high unemployment numbers are likely to continue for months or years to come, but employees affected by this phenomenon differ from those who refuse to work.

The New Testament teaches that someone who refuses to financially support his family is worse than an infidel or unbeliever. Yet, we hear countless stories of single parents or children abandoned by their biological parents, who do not step up to provide a home or the care they need.

A person who is unwilling to work, or work consistently, to provide self-support or to support those that depend on that individual for care, is in violation of God's plan for inhabiting this earth and surviving. Some aspects of culture encourage individuals not to put forth intense effort in finding and keeping a job. Millennials in great numbers are living at home with their parents into their thirties and beyond these days. Unscrupulous relationship partners prey on hard workers who will support them. Substance abuse often weakens a person's will and disrupts their interest in maintaining regular employment. All of these and other factors contribute to an unmotivated attitude among many. Proverbs 6:6 (NKJV) admonishes the slothful to learn from His handiwork in nature's design:

"Go to the ant, you sluggard! Consider her ways and be wise..."

God has provided insightful role models in creation! We should work hard like these small insects when food can be found to prepare for the coming winter of unemployment, illness, or other types of possible financial setbacks.

Most of us are not born independently wealthy, nor do we automatically become so at a certain age. Even lottery winners generally fail to hold on to their winnings – much less invest them for profit. Research suggests that an estimated 98 percent of those who win massive amounts in the lottery have lost all or most of it within two years. We are destined to work for most of our adult lives. Our attitude toward work and all our responsibilities should be one of commitment to excellence in serving the Lord, not just people.

WRATH

Anger is a common human emotion. Everyone experiences it now and then – especially when it is stoked by irresponsible or dangerous acts of others. When a reckless driver cuts in front of you and misses your car by a hair's breadth, your first impulse may be to lay on the horn. But chances are that driver knows what happened and feels no remorse. Your horn is not going to school his or her behavior and elicit an apology.

Family members incite our anger or rage by doing things we despise, possibly knowing in advance that we will get ticked off. A teen son who takes the car without permission or a daughter who talks back needs self-controlled training and discipline – not your wrath. Paul reminds us in Ephesians 4:26 (NKJV) to control our anger:

"Be angry, and do not sin": do not let the sun go down on your wrath...

Yet, culture today bombards us with media accounts of people losing their tempers and committing illegal or atrocious acts. Screaming frenzies are standard on the job, in schools, and in the public sector. Social media is filled with videos of people losing their temper and engaging in explosive arguments, with threats posted Twitter feeds and by Facebook members.

Our culture is angry – with our leaders, with each other, and with themselves. As Christians, we must remain calm and be the light on a hill that illuminates God's righteousness. Those who can hold their temper display strong character:

He who is slow to anger is better than the mighty, And he who rules his spirit than he who takes a city.
(Proverbs 16:32 NKJV)

If Christians cannot control strong emotions like rage, how can we hope to impact the culture around us with a message of peace?

PRIDE

Sometimes called the deadliest of the seven deadly sins, Bible scholars point out that Satan rebelled against God and fell from Heaven, taking a third of the heavenly host with him – due to pride:

"How you are fallen from heaven, O Lucifer, son of the morning! How you are cut down to the ground, You who weakened the nations!
(Isaiah 14:12 NKJV)

After God created Adam and Eve, Satan confronted Eve in the Garden of Eden and tempted her to eat fruit from the Tree of the Knowledge of Good and Evil by promising her that she would be like God:

> *Then the serpent said to the woman, "You will not surely die. For God knows that in the day you eat of it your eyes will be opened, and you will be like God, knowing good and evil."*
>
> (Genesis 3:4-5 NKJV)

Instead of pulling back from this offer and taking refuge in her fear of and reverence for God, Eve gave in to Satan's deception and ate the fruit, sharing it with Adam. Evidently, she was eager to become "like God." If that is not pride, what is? The wise King Solomon warns his readers against this highly destructive flaw:

> *Pride goes before destruction, and a haughty spirit before a fall.*
>
> (Proverbs 16:18 NKJV)

Here in the twenty-first century, human pride continues to reach new and shocking heights. Scientists are creating human-animal hybrids in sponsored research laboratories. People are changing their gender by rewriting birth certificates with the help of medical practitioners who prescribe drugs and perform surgery on adults and minors. Spaceships to travel the universe are being built for future expeditions. Millions of unborn babies have been legally killed since 1973, and euthanasia and assisted suicide have been embraced by our culture as life-affirming options instead of the death sentences that they are. Few consider God's laws on these and related matters. God designed us, created us, redeemed us, and saves us – we belong to Him:

Your eyes saw my substance, being yet unformed. And in Your book they all were written, The days fashioned for me, when as yet there were none of them.
(Psalms 139:16 NKJV)

On every level of society, pride is evident in a growing disrespect for self, families, communities, government – and God. People believe more and more that they can do whatever they want and escape the consequences. They boast that they know what is best for their lives despite common sense and legal limits. God has been pushed to the sidelines or even to the maintenance closet. For many, He has been forced out of modern living and relegated to a distant corner of the universe because we want to rule the world our way, not His.

We are all guilty of these and countless other sins – large and small. As Jesus taught, those who are guilty of one sin are guilty of all – and that means each one of us. If we lived individually on small islands away from each other because of our fallen nature, we would still commit sins detested by God. But living in a bustling world fueled by competition, uncontrolled passions, and greed, we are doomed to repeat the sins of our fathers and mothers until we come to the realization of the impact that culture has on each of us, no matter how public or private our existence.

Thomas grew up in a middle-class home with two busy working parents. He often watched television after school before dinner and then played video games afterward with friends. Although he passed all his school subjects, his grades could have been better. However, the main concern of his grandmother was the sense Thomas was straying for his Biblical foundation. His parents took Thomas and his younger sister Teresa to church occasionally but were not regular attenders. Thomas had a general idea of Christianity but felt no pressing interest to know more or get involved with church friends and social activities. Instead, he got hooked on TV programs with mature content that his parents weren't supervising, and his high school video game pals joked about drinking and finding girls while playing the games. When Thomas's grandmother invited him to go to church with her, he only agreed because she was buying them breakfast beforehand. Since she urged him to go to the high school Sunday school class, he obliged and was pleasantly surprised to find some cute girls there and a couple of cool guys who played sports for their school. A few weeks later, Thomas asked to go with his grandmother to church again, and a pattern was established. A year later, Thomas gave his life to the Lord. Sometimes it just takes the efforts of a caring person to intervene in a vulnerable individual's life and help them find the path to God while escaping the traps of the world's culture.

Titus spoke God's truth to the culture of his time. His message resonates with believers today as we ponder the sins of our fathers and mothers that continue to manifest in our lives, generation after generation.

In the next chapter, we will explore the biblical "fruit of the Spirit." Cultivating these blessed gifts can empower us to overcome the "deeds of the flesh" as sown into our spirits by the seeds of secular culture.

Chapter
2

The Fruit of the Spirit

But the fruit of the Spirit is love, joy, peace, longsuffering, kindness, goodness, faithfulness, gentleness, self-control. Against such there is no law. And those who are Christ's have crucified the flesh with its passions and desires. If we live in the Spirit, let us also walk in the Spirit. Let us not become conceited, provoking one another, envying one another.

(Galatians 5:22-23 NKJV)

Many people today are following special diets of one kind or another. It might be the paleo diet, the keto diet, or a nutrition plan fashioned by the American Heart Association or the American Diabetes Association. In many successful weight management plans endorsed by doctors worldwide, fruit and vegetables play an important role. Fruit is nutritious,

THE FRUIT OF THE SPIRIT

delicious, convenient, and widely available. We have learned that our fruit is filled with vitamins and minerals, numerous varieties cater to almost any appetite or eating plan. Perhaps our appetite for tasty fruit goes all the way back to the Garden of Eden, where Eve was tempted by Satan to eat the forbidden fruit from the Tree of the Knowledge of Good and Evil: *So when the woman saw that the tree was good for food, that it was pleasant to the eyes, and a tree desirable to make one wise, she took of its fruit and ate. She also gave to her husband with her, and he ate.* (Genesis 3:6 NKJV)

However, this fruit was deadly. It cost Eve – and Adam – everything that God had given them except life itself: their Garden home, their relationship with Him, and their freedom to enjoy a carefree existence. Now their lives would be filled with work, pain, and strife until Jesus came to earth many generations later to provide redemption to those who accept it.

Perhaps there is something about fruit that is irresistible, and that is why Paul writes of the "fruit of the spirit" in his letter to the church at Galatia. Many regions in this part of the world include arid or semi-arid terrain that is challenging to farm due to little water. Oasis and garden imagery offer respite and refuge in real and literary locales; thus, fruit seems to be an especially prized food group in the Middle East and other parts of the world. In the Garden of Eden, Adam and Eve gave in to Satan's temptation of earthly fruit, allowing sin to enter the world and carry down through their offspring. The original fruit proved deadly because it was eaten in disobedience to God's command.

Today, Christians are called to "crucify" our flesh with its passions and desires, to obey God fully. We are called to partake of the fruit of the Holy Spirit, as God has not prohibited these fruits, unlike the forbidden fruit in Eden: *But the fruit of the Spirit is love, joy, peace, longsuffering, kindness, goodness, faithfulness, gentleness, self-control. Against such there is no law.* (Galatians 5:22-23 NKJV)

As much as Christians try to adopt these fruitful behaviors to please God and draw others to Him, contemporary culture has distorted the meaning of these biblical values. We must learn to discern between Godly meanings of these fruits and the world's distorted use of them.

LOVE

"All you need is love," sang the world-renowned Beatles band in the late twentieth century. "Love the one you're with," crooned a pop singer at the famed Woodstock music festival. These are just two of countless popular songs that over the past seventy years or so have twisted the concept of love to mean highly individualized emotions about an extensive range of relationships – some of which the Bible brands as sinful.

Since the mid-twentieth century, when prayer was removed from schools, the birth control "pill" became widely available, and "free sex" arose as the newest youth credo. Simultaneously, the drug culture claimed increasing numbers of victims, the idea of "love" has continued to morph into whatever people decide that it should mean. Crossing traditional borders to enter the formerly forbidden territory, "love" between same-sex partners or within polyamorous groups of three or more have become commonplace and widely accepted. Love has become the byword of "woke" culture that enables and encourages expressions of physical and emotional affection between just about anyone and anything. Love in the pervading culture generally stands for self-gratification.

God's decree of love remains unchanged from the beginning of time until now – and lasts forever: *So he answered and said, " 'You shall love the LORD your God with all your heart, with all your soul, with all your strength, and with all your mind,' and 'your neighbor as yourself.' "* (Luke 10:27 NKJV)

All through the Old Testament and the New Testament, examples of right love and wrong love abound. They reveal how we should – and should not – love ourselves, others, and God.

> *"Love suffers long and is kind; love does not envy; love does not parade itself, is not puffed up; does not behave rudely, does not seek its own, is not provoked, thinks no evil; does not rejoice in iniquity, but rejoices in the truth; bears all things, believes all things, hopes all things, endures all things. Love never fails."*
>
> (I Corinthians 13:4-8 NKJV)

God shows us how to love through Jesus – His life, ministry, death, resurrection, and future hope. Any other type of love is a cheap imitation.

JOY

Today's world is full of troubles and uncertainties that can cause us to feel anxious at times. Disease, unemployment, family conflict, and many other stressful situations nibble at our faith, leaving us feeling vulnerable and afraid.

That is not how God wants us to live. When you look around at this wondrous world in which we live, at the magnificent universe God created, and the incredible future we have with God in Heaven – we should feel constant joy in being sons and daughters of the Kingdom.

Life can be difficult, and trials will come. Losses will take their toll. But as Christians, we have so much more to sustain us here on earth until we meet our Savior face to face and finally find the peace that passes understanding. *My brethren, count it all joy when you fall into various trials, knowing that the testing of your faith produces patience. But let patience have its perfect work, that you may be perfect and complete, lacking nothing. ... (James 1:2 NKJV)*

Do not let this material culture steal your joy with daily dismal news reports and frightening projections about our health and well-being. Embrace your faith with joy. God has a dazzling plan that involves you, and you have every reason to be filled with hope and happiness.

PEACE

This world is desperately searching for peace, but it is looking in all the wrong places.

Peace does not come from giving in and letting everyone have whatever they want: immigrants without rules, funds without accountability, freedoms without responsibility. That is akin to giving in to a child's tantrum to make it quiet without imparting learning or guidance.

God's peace comes from accepting His love and leading in your life: *"These things I have spoken to you, that in Me you may have peace. In the world you will have tribulation; but be of good cheer, I have overcome the world."* (John 16:33 NKJV)

Christian media and literature include numerous real accounts of believers who were tortured for their faith. Many suffered unspeakable horrors without capitulating. Witnesses claim that so many of these martyrs remained at peace during captivity, torture, and death. The only way to explain their composure is to acknowledge that their hearts trusted in God's providence, and He did not desert them in their time of need.

Peace is in short supply these days. In a world wandering further from God each day, confusion, anxiety, fear, and anger continue to grow. As Christians, our duties include helping others to find peace by serving as an example and helping to diffuse conflicts and dissension:

> *Blessed are the peacemakers, For they shall be called sons of God.*
>
> (Matthew 5:9 NKJV)

We must avoid arguments and disputes with others and encourage others to do the same. While we may have reason to disagree about something, differences of opinion should be handled graciously and lovingly to maintain peaceful relations.

Our roads are filled with enraged drivers. The courts are backed up with lawsuits. Domestic violence and child abuse reports are reaching historic levels. God's love is nowhere to be found in these events. So, we must demonstrate the peace of God. People need to know how the peace of God can keep them in line with the will of God

LONGSUFFERING

Longsuffering means to bear difficulty or challenge calmly. Instead of complaining or trying to instantly change something to make it more amenable to our needs or desires, we sometimes need to bear silently or good-naturedly a process or event that may be painful.

Suffering quietly over some time may seem wasteful to our culture when almost anything can be quickly changed to suit our appetite or comfort. But the Apostle Paul indicates in this passage that we are to bear our burdens without complaining, finding solace and respite in the Lord Jesus: *Come to Me, all you who labor and are heavy laden, and I will give you rest.* (Matthew 11:28 NKJV) No earthly yoke is too heavy to bear when we can lean on Jesus for support.

KINDNESS

Most people, saved or unsaved, understand the universal call to practice kindness toward others, and many do. But even Christians can get caught up in a frenzied culture and make rude comments to or about others. Have you ever cut in front of someone in line? Ignored a charity's plea for donations? Snapped at a store associate who was not understanding what you were trying to say?

We are all guilty of being unkind on occasion. Hopefully, we feel guilty afterward and repent, possibly making amends if the opportunity exists. Paul's epistle to the Ephesians reminded new Christians to practice kindness toward each other in following the example of Jesus: *And be kind to one another, tenderhearted, forgiving one another, even as God in Christ forgave you.* (Ephesians 4:32 NKJV)

Cutthroat politics and business deals make us feel that greedy, cruel people get ahead by stepping on others. But our Lord teaches us a different way. He is able to turn our stony hearts to hearts reflecting the love and kindness of Christ. As someone once said, the most unlovable people are the ones who need it most.

GOODNESS

> *Now as He was going out on the road, one came running, knelt before Him, and asked Him, "Good Teacher, what shall I do that I may inherit eternal life?" So Jesus said to him, "Why do you call Me good? No one is good but One, that is, God."*
>
> (Mark 10:17-18 NKJV)

How is it that Jesus asked the young man why he was calling Jesus "good"? Those who read the Bible can see that Jesus lived a good and holy life. Clearly, the crowds that followed Him could see it as well. But the young man who calls out to Jesus, "Good Teacher," is seemingly reprimanded for stating the obvious.

But was it obvious to this young man that Jesus was truly good? Or was he trying to score points with the popular traveling preacher to earn the "eternal life" that was promised? Since Jesus replied that only God is good, the implication may be that the young man did not know God well, if at all, and was more interested in a trending religious movement. We do not know for sure what Jesus meant. But we can agree that only God is good – purely good – and Jesus, being one with the Father, is likewise pure and good.

Today, we frequently hear expressions – often used in

marketing terms – about living the good life, being a good soul, or having good children. But God's meaning is far more specific: there is only one who is good – God. To be termed "good" like Him, we must be like Him. And that is something the culture does not endorse.

In fact, mainstream society claims that adultery can be "good" for marriages in trouble. It argues that abortion is "good" to give women control over their bodies. Divorce can be "good" when a couple experiences problems. God's notion of "good" is rejected, while humankind's selfish and limited considerations of "good" are extolled and pursued.

Whatever society terms as "good" should be considered suspect by Christians until they measure it against God's holy standard of goodness.

FAITHFULNESS

Loyalty, devotion, allegiance – call it what you will, the idea of faithfulness is to remain committed and dedicated to someone or something despite contrary circumstances. The culture suggests it is acceptable to switch spouses, jobs, or friends when you stop receiving from them what you feel is deserved. Sometimes, we are slighted by a boss, a spouse, or a friend and feel it is within our rights to move on. Each situation is unique, but the Bible provides plenty of principles for guiding essential decisions in these areas of life.

For example, a friend might cause a one-off rift by forgetting a critical pre-planned event. A random or infrequent lapse does not suggest the need to drop the friend unless the incidents were critical. When we think of the friendship of David and Jonathan in the Old Testament, we are in awe of their steadfast commitment to each other's well-being, even though Jonathan's father, King Saul, was pursuing David to kill him.

Being married to the same person for many years means we will see their worst side and sometimes disagree with them, as things may go wrong in their lives. Everyone falls short on occasion. You must decide if you can overlook or forgive the offense and remain committed to your marriage vows. The Bible outlines the precise parameters for divorce, so if you break your vows outside of God's laws and become unfaithful, you are sinning.

Maintaining fidelity to your employer includes not working a side job if it is prohibited by company policy. Faithfulness on the job can also mean performing your duties as expected without complaint or shirking, even if circumstances make the job demanding.

However, the culture around us waters down the quality of faithfulness to make it more comfort centered. We give up, move on, and take our fill of something or someone until we begin to feel shortchanged or restless. "Be faithful – as long as you don't have to struggle or make sacrifices," secular society suggests: *For there is no faithfulness in their mouth; their inward part is destruction; their throat is an open tomb; they flatter with their tongue.* (Psalms 5:9 NKJV)

In contrast, God is the perfect example of faithfulness – always present, never changing:

O LORD God of hosts, Who is mighty like You, O LORD? Your faithfulness also surrounds You. (Psalms 89:8 NKJV) Are you known for your faithful nature? Christians who have decided to follow Jesus must make faithfulness a characteristic of their new life.

GENTLENESS

The quality of gentleness is often equated with weakness. Many people confuse someone with a gentle demeanor as weak or a pushover. In Christian life, nothing could be further from the truth.

Humility, a manifestation of gentleness, has been defined by Christian leaders as "power under control." Followers of Jesus do not feel the need to push others around to appear stronger or better. When we demonstrate gentleness, we often allow others to go first and give them the first or best choice. We understand that everyone struggles with one or many burdens, and we will not add to that struggle by imposing more demands. Instead, we will offer what help might be needed or stand on the sidelines to allow them to excel without our help.

A gentle attitude accommodates other people. It does not

fight to get its way. Gentleness is caring, concerned, and comforting. It stands for what is right according to God's Word, but not in a forceful or controlling way.

Jesus set the perfect example of this trait: *Take My yoke upon you and learn from Me, for I am gentle and lowly in heart, and you will find rest for your souls.* (Matthew 11:29 NKJV) Jesus catered to people's needs without demanding a response. He let them think things over and come to their own decisions. There is no need for Christians to try and manipulate people into accepting Jesus as Savior. The Holy Spirit will work in the hearts of those that seek salvation.

The culture, however, echoes with dissonance. People groups of all kinds demand their rights and break laws to prove their strength by force. God gives us a spirit of gentleness to peacefully discuss important truths and rights: *A soft answer turns away wrath, but a harsh word stirs up anger.* (Proverbs 15:1 NKJV) When engaging with the surrounding culture, remember to utilize your God-given fruit of gentleness. It will be noticed in a sea of cacophony, and some will respond appreciatively.

SELF-CONTROL

Children take years to practice and master self-control. By the time we reach adulthood, we should control emotions and thoughts to respond in a Christ-like way to a culture in crisis. Self-control is an essential developmental step in our growth as new Christians. Beginning with a fundamental faith in Jesus and the Bible, believers then devote themselves to building other qualities into their lives as believers: *"But also for this very reason, giving all diligence, add to your faith virtue, to virtue knowledge, to knowledge self-control, to self-control perseverance, to perseverance godliness, to godliness brotherly kindness, and to brotherly kindness love."* (II Peter 1:5-7 NKJV) Self-control is necessary, as those who are Christians will face trials of many kinds. We must be prepared to handle them in a self-controlled way. Giving in to intense passions and emotions can hinder a believer's faith and damage their testimony. There is no place for malice, rage, lust, or other sinful feelings and actions in a Christian's life.

The culture, on the other hand, makes excuses for people who lack self-control. Drug addicts are provided homes and clean needles in some regions of the country. Teens are given access to free birth control, including surgical procedures. Terminally ill patients are assisted in dying rather than encouraged to deal with a chronic health condition. Some convicts receive light court sentences – and then resume their criminal activities upon release.

A young single mother named Saundra had been mistreated by everyone she had lived with, from foster parents to the father of her young son. Disheartened and disillusioned, Saundra felt that no one cared about her, and she began caring little about herself. From drug use to a string of boyfriends and a handful of jobs that did not work out, Saundra felt like a misfit in the culture that seemingly approved of the way she lived. At a food pantry where she could get some free groceries due to her limited income, a thirty-four-year-old married mom of two kids who were handing out cartons of food noticed Saundra's downcast face and quiet demeanor.

"Everything okay?" Janelle asked.

Surprised by the volunteer's interest, Saundra just nodded and said, "Yeah."

"Do you have a couple minutes for a cup of coffee over there?" Janelle pointed to an area with several tables where a few workers and clients relaxed over free coffee and hot chocolate.

"Sure," Saundra said.

As the two ladies got to know each other over their hot beverages, Janelle offered to help Saundra find work. "I know a small office where you could help with filing and organizing supplies," she offered. Saundra applied and got the job. Janelle stayed in touch by phone and text to answer questions and advise when Saundra asked for it. They got together weekly for lunch and to share updates. Janelle explained her challenges with one son, who had been diagnosed with ADHD. Saundra offered a few tips that her sister had learned when raising a son with the same diagnosis. In the months that followed, the women bonded, and Saundra met a coworker that invited her to church, where she was soon attending regularly and getting to know other church members while volunteering and socializing. Her son enjoyed the Sunday school classes for his age group. In time, Saundra was promoted to office assistant, and the following year she was promoted again to office manager – a long line of successes initiated in part by the kindness of a compassionate volunteer who demonstrated the fruits of the Spirit.

God holds us to a just standard in living holy lives, and He wants us to reach out and help others find Him as well. We will never be perfect, but we can do our best and rely on God's help, along with the kindness of strangers, to set goals and become the people that please and honor God.

The fruit of the Spirit is available to every believer – in contrast to the reckless freedoms of a lawless society. As you make choices each day, consider which fruits you will enjoy – the forbidden kind offered by society or the blessed kind provided by God? Choose whose law you will follow – God's or man's.

Chapter

3

Our Citizenship Is in Heaven

For our citizenship is in heaven, from which we also
eagerly wait for the Savior, the Lord Jesus Christ...
(Philippians 3:20 NKJV)

The current cost of an application for US citizenship is approximately $725. That is not much, considering all the perks resulting from being a citizen of one of the greatest nations on earth. When you add up the benefits of living permanently in this country for a lifetime of seventy or eighty-plus years, they total a hefty sum: lifetime employment opportunities, potential healthcare coverage, law enforcement, a judicial process, in many cases, a free or affordable education, extensive personal freedoms, and many, many more.

In comparison, eternal citizenship in Heaven is free. You do not have to pay a penny to enjoy a literal paradise existence. You will not need most of the material benefits mentioned above. As a believer in Jesus Christ, redeemed from your sins by His blood, you are guaranteed a mansion in the only perfect community in the universe. God will meet all your needs in ways that are greater than you can imagine and vastly better than the most luxurious gated community lifestyle you could ever want here on earth.

In Heaven, your security, comfort, well-being, and future are provided by God. In fact, He preplanned your existence before you were even conceived by your parents. He also created Heaven simultaneously as He created earth: *"In the beginning God created the heavens and the earth. The earth was without form and void, and darkness was on the face of the deep.*

> *And the Spirit of God was hovering over the face of the waters. Then God said, "Let there be light"; and there was light. And God saw the light, that it was good; and God divided the light from the darkness. God called the light Day, and the darkness He called Night. So the evening and the morning were the first day. Then God said, "Let there be a firmament in the midst of the waters, and let it divide the waters from the waters." Thus God made the firmament, and divided the waters which were under the firmament from the waters which were above the firmament; and it was so. And God called the firmament Heaven. So the evening and the morning were the second day.*
>
> (Genesis 1:1-8 NKJV)

Just as the earth was to be our temporary physical home for thousands of years as God's plan for humanity unfolded, Heaven was ordained as our eternal spiritual home following the separation of individual bodies and spirits with physical death and our departure from this earthly realm. While many of us can reasonably expect to live up to a hundred years or a little more at most, we know with certainty that our eternity will be spent in Heaven – if we are redeemed by the Savior's blood. Those who do not accept His precious gift of forgiveness of sins and spiritual salvation will spend eternity in a dark state of abandonment and suffering – Hell.

In today's world, God has been banned from public life, while humanism reigns supreme. From the time of Christ through the Renaissance a few hundred years ago, God was depicted and accepted as being at the center of our world and ruler of the universe. With the progress of science and the rise of evolutionary theory, God is no longer needed by our culture. Man has been crowed the Supreme Leader of this world and beyond. Therefore, whatever man wants, he will be encouraged to strive and achieve it. Rather than being urged to pray for God's guidance, he is incited to claim whatever brings instant gratification.

Culture Tells Us to Live for Today

Popular songs, television series, and award-winning films urge us to live in the moment and not worry about tomorrow. While there are times when we need to deal with imminent issues or emergencies, our overall approach to life should be to focus on the eternal horizon, not on the side trails of the moment.

We are bombarded by advertisements wherever we look – computer, smartphone, television, movie screen, audio devices. Marketable goods promise health, wealth, happiness, and ease if we just buy their touted products. We are told to trade in a four-year-old vehicle that is running just fine for a brand-new model that will add $200 to the monthly budget, not to mention an increase in car insurance premiums. Sell your current middle-class home with a half-paid mortgage for a pricier version that you can barely afford and a heftier mortgage payment that now extends another fifteen years.

Then, the world reminds us that we can steep our lives in indulgences of every kind – fashion clothing, country club memberships, expensive vacations, restaurant dining – whatever you want, it's yours for the asking – and payment, of course.

The result of this grandiose lifestyle approach is a monthly budget that is ready to crash, especially if you lose your job during a personal or local crisis. But our comfort culture reassures you that everything is fine. You can get a low-interest credit card to pay off your debt and make slow repayments over time. Or you can declare bankruptcy, wipe your financial slate clean, and start all over again in a never-ending cycle.

Your US citizenship is never in jeopardy if you do not turn traitor by colluding with foreign powers, and most citizens are unlikely to do so. Concentrate your efforts on keeping up with the Joneses rather than Jesus, and everything will work in your favor. You can enjoy a cushy lifestyle with minimal effort, possibly supported by the government, at little to no risk. That is what life is all about, society tells us. Live for the moment, squeeze every drop of living out of your income and opportunities, and do not worry about tomorrow, because tomorrow never comes, right?

Wrong! The Bible frequently speaks of the future and how Christians must prepare for it. We are never exhorted to live in the moment and settle into a complacent attitude. Unfortunately, we are tempted to do just that. Everyone else is savoring life's pleasures, so why shouldn't we? The Bible does not say it is a crime to be happy, does it? Nor does it chastise the wealthy or a luxurious lifestyle. But the Bible does have plenty to say in comparing this current life to the coming future life and weighing the temporary hedonism of this world against the pure joys of the next.

> *"But this I say, brethren, the time is short, so that from now on even those who have wives should be as though they had none, those who weep as though they did not weep, those who rejoice as though they did not rejoice, those who buy as though they did not possess, and those who use this world as not misusing it. For the form of this world is passing away."*
>
> (I Corinthians 7:29-31 NKJV)

The Apostle Paul's letter to the church at Corinth underscores the importance of believers living with a focus on God rather than being deeply rooted in this life. Of course, we must maintain our relationships and responsibilities, but we must also put care for God's Kingdom and our role in that Kingdom at a high place in our lives.

More and more, we are seeing signs of the end times prophesied in the Bible coming to pass. One day soon, Jesus will return to rapture believers out of this life, leaving the world to its foretold fate of darkness and destruction. At that time, Christians will be grateful to escape their earthly bonds and embrace their eternal citizenship in Heaven with God as our King.

THE JOURNEY AND THE BATTLE

> *"And do not be conformed to this world, but be transformed by the renewing of your mind, that you may prove what is that good and acceptable and perfect will of God."*
> (Romans 12:2 NKJV)

If you have visited a foreign country, it may seem like a strange, exotic place at first. But if you have met citizens of the country previously or have extensively researched the nation and its people, you might feel at home sooner than later. Arriving at a place you have longed to see, you will likely experience joy, excitement, and a sense of fulfillment.

We may well have the same response when we reach

Heaven's gates. As followers of Jesus Christ, we wait for the rest of our lives from the moment of salvation to reach our heavenly home and ultimate destination. Meanwhile, we put on the whole armor of God to fight spiritual battles and spread the Gospel to every corner of the world, whether by missions' work or donations of support.

This world is not our permanent home. We are passing through on a day-by-day basis. Although we can put down roots and establish families, everything should be done in the role of Christian, from setting a Christ-like example to doing the work that God has assigned each believer.

Along the way, there will be countless temptations, as noted above, in observations about worldly culture. The secular focus is on temporal interests; Christians are to address eternal issues. We are in contradiction with our culture – in fact, we are at war with it: *"Beloved, I beg you as sojourners and pilgrims, abstain from fleshly lusts which war against the soul."* (I Peter 2:11 NKJV)

The human body is made of mud – literally, earth and water, as described in the Genesis account of creation. It deteriorates and decays over time. But the human spirit has been transmitted to the flesh in the literal breath of God. If we make our earthly selves the focus of life, everything we gain will be lost at death. But if we follow a spiritual life in Christ, our rewards will only fully be recognized and claimed in Heaven: *"For he who sows to his flesh will of the flesh reap corruption, but he who sows to the Spirit will of the Spirit reap everlasting life.* " (Galatians 6:8 NKJV) The flesh is seduced by worldly desires – they are strong and many, conceived by Satan and manifested by demons.

Spiritual warfare is a constant threat to our faith and abilities: *"For we do not wrestle against flesh and blood, but against principalities, against powers, against the rulers of the darkness of this age, against spiritual hosts of wickedness in the heavenly places."* (Ephesians 6:12 NKJV)

It is hard to understand exactly what these dark powers represent. But we know that our thoughts are often overshadowed by temptation. Doubt can arise to confront us at our weakest moments. The Adversary, Satan, has a host of armies ready to do his bidding so that we may feel the battle is lost before we can even lift a shield. But God has provided all the weaponry needed to prepare us to win the battle by following His leadership: *"Therefore take up the whole armor of God, that you may be able to withstand in the evil day, and having done all, to stand. Stand therefore, having girded your waist with truth, having put on the breastplate of righteousness, and having shod your feet with the preparation of the gospel of peace; above all, taking the shield of faith with which you will be able to quench all the fiery darts of the wicked one. And take the helmet of salvation, and the sword of the Spirit, which is the word of God; praying always with all prayer and supplication in the Spirit, being watchful to this end with all perseverance and supplication for all the saints."* (Ephesians 6:13-18 NKJV)

In the Old Testament, God rescued the children of Israel from Egyptian bondage, and then He led them into the Promised Land. Although it took forty years (due to their disobedience) for what should have been a journey of a couple of weeks, reaching their long-awaited destination was a dream come true for generations of Abraham's descendants who had been slaves to a foreign ruler for 400 years. When they reached the borders of their promised nation, they were given the task of reclaiming their birthright from the occupying inhabitants. This required years of warfare, competently led by Moses' military assistant, Joshua. In time, the Israelites resettled the land according to the tribal dispensation preplanned by God. Celebrations, feasts, and commemorations, along with monuments, marked their progress and charted their victory.

This exciting illustration of God keeping His promise to the chosen people and enabling them to reach the land of their forefathers prepares us for our long journey toward Heaven. It will take time, there will be battles, but the arrival will be worth it – far beyond our most vivid dreams and expectations.

HEAVEN'S CITIZENSHIP

Becoming a citizen confers the full rights and responsibilities of belonging to a sovereign nation. You are a fully recognized member of that country, having earned or, in some manner, paid for your passage and your "application" for citizenship.

However, the most unique quality of heavenly citizenship

is that all fees and requirements are waived. The only thing you must do is believe that Jesus died for your sins, accept His precious gift, and establish a lasting relationship with Him and other citizens in his Kingdom.

What makes Heaven so special that we cannot wait to spend eternity there?

First, it is God's dwelling place:

The LORD is in His holy temple, The LORD's throne is in heaven...

(Psalms 11:4 NKJV)

Christians who love God wait a lifetime to be with Him in Heaven. As described in Revelation, it is a beautiful and wondrous place, holy and pure.

Second, Satan / Lucifer no longer resides in Heaven. He and a third of the angels who followed him were cast from Heaven when they rebelled. Heaven is free of their influence:

"How you are fallen from heaven, O Lucifer, son of the morning! How you are cut down to the ground, You who weakened the nations!

(Isaiah 14:12 NKJV)

Third, we will receive our just rewards:

…but lay up for yourselves treasures in heaven, where neither moth nor rust destroys and where thieves do not break in and steal.

(Matthew 6:20 NKJV)

Fourth, we will reunite with Christian loved ones and meet other Christians in God's family: " *After these things I looked, and behold, a great multitude which no one could number, of all nations, tribes, peoples, and tongues, standing before the throne and before the Lamb, clothed with white robes, with palm branches in their hands, and crying out with a loud voice, saying, "Salvation belongs to our God who sits on the throne, and to the Lamb!"* (Revelation 7:9-10 NKJV)

Fifth, God will eliminate our suffering and care for all our needs: " *They shall neither hunger anymore nor thirst anymore; the sun shall not strike them, nor any heat; for the Lamb who is in the midst of the throne will shepherd them and lead them to living fountains of waters. And God will wipe away every tear from their eyes. "* (Revelation 7:16-17 NKJV)

Sixth, God will assume control of this world:

"The kingdoms of this world have become the kingdoms of our Lord and of His Christ, and He shall reign forever and ever!"

(Revelation 11:15 NKJV)

Seventh, Satan is to be cast into the lake of burning fire forever, and the unsaved will be judged: *"The devil, who deceived them, was cast into the lake of fire and brimstone where the beast and the false prophet are. And they will be tormented day and night forever and ever. Then I saw a great white throne and Him who sat on it, from whose face the earth and the heaven fled away. And there was found no place for them. And I saw the dead, small and great, standing before God, and books were opened. And another book was opened, which is the Book of Life. And the dead were judged according to their works, by the things which were written in the books. The sea gave up the dead who were in it, and Death and Hades delivered up the dead who were in them. And they were judged, each one according to his works. Then Death and Hades were cast into the lake of fire. This is the second death. And anyone not found written in the Book of Life was cast into the lake of fire.* (Revelation 20:10-15 NKJV)

Finally, God will destroy the former heaven and earth and create newness in their place:

> *"Now I saw a new heaven and a new earth, for the first heaven and the first earth had passed away. Also there was no more sea. Then I, John, saw the holy city, New Jerusalem, coming down out of heaven from God, prepared as a bride adorned for her husband. And I heard a loud voice from heaven saying, "Behold, the tabernacle of God is with men, and He will dwell with them, and they shall be His people. God Himself will be with them and be their God. And God will wipe away every tear from their eyes;*

there shall be no more death, nor sorrow, nor crying. There shall be no more pain, for the former things have passed away."

(Revelation 21:1-4 NKJV)

Nowadays, you hear many people, including celebrities, mocking the idea of Heaven and Hell, and joking that some cannot wait to join their friends in Hell for a party. Others criticize the Bible's Heaven as "too boring."

A teenager named Jake was cruising around the neighborhood with his gang pal Benny one night. Benny was driving his girlfriend's car, although he did not have a current driver's license. Both were smoking pot and laughing at the kids at school who worked hard to earn passing grades and hoped to go to college.

"I don't want anything to do with school," Benny said, blowing smoke rings while steering the car through a deserted alley.

"Me either," Jake dutifully agreed, although he knew high school graduation would make his parents happy. "And none of that church crap either," he added before taking a deep puff.

"That's just somethin' the old folks preach at us to make us behave," Benny giggled. "Ain't none of it real."

"You've got that right," Jake said, slowly releasing the puff he had just taken. "Ain't nothin' more real than this." He held up the joint in his fingers as both boys guffawed. Neither had any idea that they were on track to miss out on salvation and the most perfect life imaginable.

God's glorious New Jerusalem will be the final abiding place of Christian believers. Compare the descriptions of this magnificent city in Revelation 21 with any earthly city you can think of. Is a temporary life of self-indulgence on earth worth risking an eternal existence in the presence of God?

Chapter
4

Called to Be Saints

*As for the saints who are on the earth, "They are the
excellent ones, in whom is all my delight."*
(Psalms 16:3 NKJV)

If you have ever visited another country, you probably soon
saw differences between the tourists and the citizens. Visitors
who spend a short time in the region often see the surface aspects of the nation, whether good or bad, and they do not always have the opportunity to become immersed in the culture.
While a vacation or business trip can be pleasant, we often find
ourselves thinking, "There is no place like home."

The same is true for Christians in this world. Global culture in general and US culture specifically does not welcome or
support Christians. We are criticized, judged, dismissed, and
sometimes punished as the secular world tries to ignore or destroy us through Satan's influence. Being born again requires

belief in the Lord Jesus Christ, as well as water baptism and being filled with the Holy Spirit. These actions prepare us for the next world with God.

Throughout history, we have heard stories about long-suffering religious folk and have come to think of "saints" as near-perfect people who became martyrs of the Christian faith. However, that is not an accurate representation. The Bible refers to those who trust God as saints in both the Old Testament and the New Testament:

Oh, fear the LORD, you His saints! There is no want to those who fear Him.
(Psalms 34:9 NKJV)

God promises to protect all of His saints. He has chosen us for fellowship and spiritual intimacy. The Bible is full of encouragement for the saints who follow Jesus and live according to the word of God.

What does it mean to be a saint in God's Kingdom – both here on earth and in Heaven? Can anyone be a saint, or only the most righteous believers? We will consider the history of God's people and their sainthood as represented in the Bible in terms of a traveler's metaphor. We begin this life as transitory visitors and move through the world as global travelers. But one day, we will become permanent citizens of Heaven as we reach our eternal destination.

TENT DWELLERS

From the beginning of creation, God has provided homes for his children. The first couple was given a beautiful paradise, the Garden of Eden, to enjoy without effort or fear. But when Adam and Eve disobeyed God in eating the forbidden fruit, He evicted them from the Garden, and their descendants soon scattered throughout the region we now call the Middle East, particularly Israel. Although God designated the offspring of Adam and Eve as His chosen people who would be known as His saints, they had much to learn in their earthly adventures. God chose patriarchs to head these favored tribes, beginning with Abraham and continuing through Abraham's son Isaac – rejecting Ishmael, Abraham's firstborn son by the bondwoman Hagar – and ensuing through Jacob's family line of twelve sons. All were among God's chosen people, but not all lived exactly saintly lives.

These subsequent generations lived in temporary tents as they roamed the area and settled near fertile pastures and water sources for their herds and flocks, which in those times was their way of making a living, equivalent to holding a job in our day. They moved around as necessary to keep their herds well cared for, ensuring the survival and well-being of the nomadic people descended from the first couple. In that era, humans increased their knowledge of God and experienced growth in their faith as he provided for their needs and expanding clans.

Eventually, the chosen people localized in the vicinity of Canaan when Abram (later, Abraham) had been called by God to settle. Instead of building cities, God's people continued to live in tents, a symbolic reminder of their temporary and tentative residency on this earth. Later, Abraham's grandson and son of Isaac, Jacob, moved away and returned with two wives and twelve children. After that, his son Joseph was sold into Egyptian slavery by jealous brothers. This tragic event was part of God's plan to prepare His people for their future.

When a famine arose in Canaan, the patriarch Jacob sent his sons to Egypt to buy food, where God had prepared the nation for the future famine – with the "sold" brother Joseph now ruling Egypt as second in command to the pharaoh. As part of God's patriarchal line, Joseph was able to not only save Egypt during the crisis but also preserve his family and several generations of descendants who would become God's saints in the making. Thus, God brought good out of evil, as Joseph informed his brothers: *But as for you, you meant evil against me; but God meant it for good, in order to bring it about as it is this day, to save many people alive.* (Genesis 50:20 NKJV)

After Joseph died, for four hundred years, the Israelites labored as slaves in Egypt. They were not actually citizens of the land, as they did not receive benefits of citizenship but instead worked to support the nation's population and rulers. Having lost their residency in Canaan, God's people now had to wait for a redeemer – a promise God had given in the Garden of Eden and which would now be fulfilled initially by Moses, and ultimately, by Jesus.

A series of events orchestrated by God forced Pharaoh to release the Israelites to return to their homeland, which they reached only after forty years of wilderness wandering – another reminder of their temporary resident status. However, then they had to fight the Canaanites to reclaim their territory. For a time, they would still be tent dwellers until they received their inheritance of the Promised Land:

> *And now the LORD your God has given rest to your brethren, as He promised them; now therefore, return and go to your tents and to the land of your possession, which Moses the servant of the LORD gave you on the other side of the Jordan.*
>
> (Joshua 22:4 NKJV)

With God's help, the Israelites were able to resettle their homeland and establish a legacy in fulfilling their covenant with the Lord. Finally, they could begin living more like saints, as they practiced consistent faith in and obedience to God's commandments. Though imperfect, they realized that as God's chosen people, they were called to a life of moral and ethical principles based on the Ten Commandments given by Moses to guide their lives. They were learning hard lessons about the necessity of obeying God and ignoring the wicked communities around them.

Over time, the Israelites built walled towns and cities. While this process took place, they continued living in tents, especially those in rural areas. But trouble from nearby nations continued to confront them. Time after time, God's people were forced to repent of turning from the Lord to worship false idols and drifting from their sainthood status. Time after time, God delivered his people through leaders hand-picked for the purpose:

> *Then the LORD gave Israel a deliverer, so that they escaped from under the hand of the Syrians; and the children of Israel dwelt in their tents as before.*
> (2 Kings 13:5 NKJV)

Finally, God raised prophets and kings to rule over the people and maintain the Biblical standards of spiritual excellence provided by God. Under King David, Israel's second ruler, the city of Jerusalem was established as the nation's capital, and many people lived in permanent houses within the city walls. This era of their history offers a micro-glimpse of God's plan of holy living for all believers. They would live within secure boundaries in permanent homes, no longer just tents, and obey as well as support their Godly ruler, King David, a forerunner of Jesus as our ultimate and perfect King.

TRAVELERS

The Israelites had already experienced a period of exile while in Egyptian bondage for four hundred years. They also had wandered in the wilderness for another forty years. They understood the hardship and deprivation of living independent of secular communities. Thanks to Moses, their faith in God was revived when they entered the Promised Land and embraced their status as God's chosen people, making him first in their lives through worship, petition, and service. Hundreds of years later, King David's psalms recite the Israelites' praise for God and hope in his redemption. For a time, the Israelites lived like true saints of the Jewish faith as an example of separateness from surrounding nations and as a reminder not to fall back into sinful lifestyles: *I will hear what God the LORD will speak, for He will speak peace to His people and to His saints; but let them not turn back to folly.* (Psalms 85:8 NKJV)

In return, the people claimed God's promises of protection and deliverance:

> *You who love the LORD, hate evil! He preserves the souls of His saints; He delivers them out of the hand of the wicked.*
> (Psalms 97:10 NKJV)

But being human, the saints who lived under God's law began to stray from it. They adopted unbiblical attitudes and practices, worshipping false gods, and abandoning God's laws. God allowed this for an extended time, with the Israelites vacillating between holy obedience and sinful disobedience.

Finally, God gave them over to Babylonian captivity, and His lost people became travelers again, carried into exile by their enemies. There, they repented of their sinful acts and begged for God's forgiveness. Eventually, they were allowed to return to Jerusalem and rebuild the city, and saint-like living resumed. The history of the Chosen People is a roller-coaster series of events. Just as their relationship with God vacillated, so did their life experiences. Because of their infidelity to God, they were generally unsuccessful in putting down permanent roots as citizens of the Promised Land.

Hundreds of years later, when God sent His Son, Jesus, to draw the people back to their spiritual roots and saintly lives, many responded—and Christianity was born. Gentile saints joined Jewish saints in proclaiming Jesus as Messiah. For about a generation, the new young faith thrived and grew in Jerusalem and began spreading throughout the Middle East and Europe. The Apostle John experienced a vision about the future of the New Jerusalem, increasing the joy and hope of God's saints for spending eternity with God in a permanent, secure location. Instead of tents, they would dwell in mansions. Instead of prophets and kings, God would be their ruler. Their work as saints would be acknowledged and rewarded. But there was one more journey to take before the re-establishment of Israel as the permanent land for the Chosen People.

In AD 70, the Roman General Titus sacked Jerusalem and sent its residents into global exile. Many were taken to Rome, where they were tortured and killed. Others escaped to distant lands where their descendants would be born and die. God's saints no longer had a permanent country of citizenship to call their own, and many wandered from their faith. Others remained committed to serving God.

In fulfillment of Bible prophecy, Israel was reborn in a single day – May 14, 1948, when it was declared an official, internationally recognized country. Before and since that time, Jewish people from around the world have abandoned their temporal homes to return to the land of their ancestors – a nation that is both a spiritual and physical permanent home.

Christians, however, do not feel the need to live in Israel currently. They know from Bible prophecies that the New Jerusalem that God will create will one day become their permanent home. Now they are legal citizens and permanent residents of various countries, but their true allegiance is to God and the future place Jesus is preparing for His saints:

> *But the saints of the Most High shall receive the kingdom, and possess the kingdom forever, even forever and ever.*
> (Daniel 7:18 NKJV)

SAINTS AND CITIZENS

Today, there are an estimated 200 countries in the world. Most include Christians among their citizens. However, there is no single country that is labeled a "Christian" nation. Although the United States was established on Christian principles of the founders, our country has, from its inception, welcomed people from around the world who practice any religious faith, or none, to visit our country, and if conditions warrant, to become citizens.

God's Kingdom is spiritual in nature, without physical boundaries. It is a community of Christian believers who share church membership, Bible fellowship, and spiritual communion in person or online to support each other in beliefs and behaviors. Christians share a kinship that transcends bloodline, race, or ethnicity. We belong to the family of God and are part of a timeless, worldwide community of Christ-followers who will one day be part of God's Kingdom in Heaven and on earth:

All Your works shall praise You, O LORD, And Your saints shall bless You.

(Psalms 145:10 NKJV)

As believers and followers of Jesus Christ, we are called to live according to the Bible's teachings. Although legal citizens of various countries, we are not – or should not be – spiritual citizens of this secular world. We are called to be separate and to live as saints of God, as the Apostle Paul indicates in his letter to the Roman church:

To all who are in Rome, beloved of God, called to be saints: Grace to you and peace from God our Father and the Lord Jesus Christ.

(Romans 1:7 NKJV)

Paul gives a similar greeting to the church at Corinth:

To the church of God which is at Corinth, to those who are sanctified in Christ Jesus, called to be saints, with all who

in every place call on the name of Jesus Christ our Lord,
both theirs and ours:

(I Corinthians 1:2 NKJV)

Notice that Paul calls "all" who are "beloved of God" are "called to be saints" in the Roman letter and "those who are sanctified in Christ Jesus, called to be saints, with all who in every place call on the name of Jesus Christ our Lord..." in his letter to the Corinthians. There is no suggestion that only some believers can or should be saints; all believers should live saintly lives to honor our Lord and Savior. The Bible shows us how to do that, no matter our background, skills, or limitations.

Today, whether you are a tourist, a permanent resident, or a citizen in any region of the world, as a born-again believer in Jesus Christ, you are a bona fide citizen in God's Kingdom. Your saintly status is confirmed, and your heavenly citizenship is secure. What does that mean for the average believer in the 21st century?

SAINTS SHOULD BE SEPARATE FROM THE WORLD.

As ambassadors of Christ, believers must live their faith through the example of their lives. We are called apart from the world and should not participate in its wickedness and foolishness. Beginning with the Ten Commandments and throughout the Old Testament and New Testament, God has given us the rules, precepts, and guidance we need to be faithful followers that live differently from those who do not know God.

But fornication and all uncleanness or covetousness, let it not even be named among you, as is fitting for saints...
                                        (Ephesians 5:3 NKJV)

From the day we accept Christ as Redeemer, our lives should diverge from the worldly practices we used to do, so that everyone can see we are now different from and behave better than the world around us by honoring God and keeping Him first in our lives, as Paul reminds the new Christians in Rome:

And do not be conformed to this world, but be transformed by the renewing of your mind, that you may prove what is that good and acceptable and perfect will of God.
                                        (Romans 12:2 NKJV)

Daily prayer, Bible reading, and church membership help believers to grow in faith and to develop saint-like behavior that can influence others for the Lord.

SAINTS HAVE DUTIES TO PERFORM.

Saving faith is the most critical decision you will ever make in this world. When you commit your life to follow Jesus and serve God, your eternal future and heavenly citizenship are secured.

However, while dwelling in temporary earthly tents awaiting our permanent home in Heaven, there is much we can do to share Christ with the world that so badly needs Him.

Fortunately, God will ensure that we have everything needed for the assigned tasks, specifically from the Bible:

> *"…for the equipping of the saints for the work of ministry, for the edifying of the body of Christ…*
>
> (Ephesians 4:12 NKJV)

Saints are to serve as ministers, caring for other believers in need. We must share the Gospel with the unsaved by supporting or participating in ministries of various kinds. We must also build up, or edify, the body of Christ via church membership and service by using the talents and skills that God has given each of us.

We are also called to pray for each other as saints:

> *And the smoke of the incense, with the prayers of the saints, ascended before God from the angel's hand.*
>
> (Revelation 8:4 NKJV)

Prayer is powerful. It is the most important thing we can do as saints, because prayer transcends physical acts of kindness when we cannot do something or be in a particular place. Wherever we are, we can offer prayers of gratitude, petition, hope, and repentance. We must pray routinely to God, asking for help and direction. He is always listening, and He will answer the prayers of His saints.

SAINTS WILL FACE TRIALS.

Becoming a Christian believer does not make life easier. In fact, your life could become more difficult. Satan is busy at work, trying to keep unbelievers from accepting Jesus as Savior. The Evil One also tries to discourage the saints, because if he cannot keep them from attaining salvation, he will try to disrupt their efforts to lead others to Christ. You can expect trials, problems, disappointments, and setbacks as your Christian life becomes more substantial.

Ultimately, the saints will someday face the Satan-supported Antichrist in battle:

It was granted to him to make war with the saints and to overcome them. And authority was given him over every tribe, tongue, and nation.
(Revelation 18:7 NKJV)

Being a saint in the world today is an everyday battle. However, we have joy as it also a God-honoring lifetime commitment that will last for eternity and culminate in permanent citizenship in Heaven while receiving our final judgment and reward.

A middle-aged woman got off the bus and trudged down the street to her low-income apartment. She had lived in this area most of her life and knew many residents, but few were friendly. They kept to themselves despite Susan's efforts to offer kindness by bringing over a homemade cake or informing them of new community services like a children's health clinic and a food bank. She had been awakened several times throughout the years by loud fighting in the surrounding apartments, sirens shrieking as police cars and EMS vehicles pulled into the street. It seemed like nothing ever changed. "Lord help me," she prayed, "I'm tired, and nothing I do seems to help anybody."

Past retirement age, Susan volunteered once a week at a local daycare to wash and sterilize children's toys. She also crocheted baby hats for winter that she donated to the hospital's neonatal unit. From her meager pension, Susan gave as much as she could afford to ministries she believed were reaching the unsaved, despite a lack of confirmation or certainty.

"Lord, I'm tired," she prayed more and more frequently as disillusionment set in.

One night a neighbor knocked at the door, and when Susan answered, she asked, "Could I go to church with you this Sunday? I've heard you over here singing hymns, and I noticed how you try to help everyone. I've been miserable a long time, and I need God to work in me the way He is working in you."

Susan was delighted and agreed for the woman named Stella to accompany her to church the following Sunday morning. Stella did not mind taking the bus.

"Thank you, Lord," Susan prayed that night and the many

nights that followed. She was grateful not only for God bring-ing Stella into her life and into His church, but also for releasing Susan from the fear of failure and the pain of disappointment as she looked forward more than ever to her heaven-bound destiny.

Our earthly future as believers should be filled with joy and hope as we live saintly lives in a secular culture. But the fulfillment of that hope will come at a cost. If we are to give up these earthly tents of temporary residence to claim the heav-enly mansions of eternity with God, we must take up our cross daily and follow in our Savior's footsteps:

> *Here is the patience of the saints; here are those who keep*
> *the commandments of God and the faith of Jesus.*
> (Revelation 14:12 NKJV)

Chapter

5

Intimacy with God

*Be still, and know that I am God; I will be exalted among
the nations, I will be exalted in the earth!*
                                        (Psalms 46:10 NKJV)

Most cultures in today's world have heard about God in
one way or another. In Western societies, understanding and belief in the Judeo-Christian God have been prevalent
for nearly 2,000 years. As the Gospel has been shared throughout the globe, other regions have been introduced to the God
of the Bible, with many people accepting Jesus as Lord and
Savior. Some countries identify Christianity as their primary
religion, while Israel embraces Judaism as its root faith. Other
cultures, however, condemn Christianity and persecute the followers of Jesus.

Some people recognize the virtues of Christianity and
admire its tenets of belief, but not all accept the doctrinal

principles or embrace God as Father, Son, and Holy Spirit. In fact, most people who acknowledge Christianity at all either ignore the Bible's teachings or adapt them to their preferred interpretation and practice. We can see this in individuals we know and specific groups and organizations who claim to be Christians yet deny critical aspects of the Bible. Believing that a single God presides over the universe is the first step of faith, but it is not enough:

> *You believe that there is one God. You do well. Even the demons believe—and tremble!*
> (James 2:19 NKJV)

Those who are genuinely called to salvation understand the enormity of the gift that God offers and bestows on those who trust Him. They are in awe of God sending His one and only Son to show us how to live and then pay for humanity's sins by dying on the cross before rising again to give us hope through His resurrection. How can anyone who fully grasps God's salvation and promise of eternity take the Christian faith so lightly? Sadly, many are called, but few are chosen.

Although many people claim to be Christians, they often hide their faith due to cultural pressure and rejection of the Bible's principles. Faithful followers of Jesus are recognizable by their beliefs and actions, as Jesus points out:

> *Therefore by their fruits you will know them.*
> (Matthew 7:20 NKJV)

If you are unsure whether someone is a Christian or living a Christian lifestyle commanded by God, reflect on the fruits produced by various actions and behaviors. The Old Testament teaches us the most essential response to God through the words of Samuel the prophet:

> *So Samuel said: "Has the LORD as great delight in burnt offerings and sacrifices, As in obeying the voice of the LORD? Behold, to obey is better than sacrifice, and to heed than the fat of rams.*
>
> (I Samuel 15:22 NKJV)

It is not enough to dress in our finery for church services to put on a show of religious fervor. Our hearts must be in tune with God as we develop an intimate relationship with Him. Just as you cultivate a special relationship with the person with whom you fall in love and want to marry, it is more important to develop a close, intimate relationship with God – who has created you, sustains you, redeems you, and is preparing an eternal home for you in Heaven with Him? Everything that God does for us surpasses anything another human can do to show love or make you happy.

As you think about getting closer to God, consider the parallels to loving family relationships here on earth. In some respects, they can serve as guidance in helping you build a stable relationship of faith in God, who loves you and seeks fellowship with you.

PHYSICAL CLOSENESS

Spending time with someone you care about is one of the main ways to establish physical and emotional connections. God is spirit, and we cannot perceive Him through the five senses of sight, sound, smell, touch, or taste. But we can experience spiritual closeness with God by spending time in the Bible, His holy book, that is actually similar to a long love letter or series of letters to someone much loved as a source of information and inspiration.

Daily Bible readings will help you to understand the mind of God and His plan for humanity, beginning in Genesis and proceeding through Revelation. Over and over, you will see God's love for you, and all of us described clearly and emphatically. Is there any more straightforward way He could show how much he cares for us than through the words conveyed by His hand-picked leaders, prophets, and apostles? Reading just a chapter a day will increase your insight into God's character and build your faith and trust in His providence. Every relationship needs security and stability to survive, and the Bible provides that for believers in a tangible way experienced through prayer to God and fellowship with believers.

You also can and should join a church of a denomination that endorses Bible doctrine as unerring truth by exercising worship and praise that you are comfortable with. Regular attendance is vital to connect with God's people.

…not forsaking the assembling of ourselves together, as is the manner of some, but exhorting one another, and so much the more as you see the Day approaching.
(Hebrews 10:25 NKJV)

Just as you get acquainted with a love interest's friends and relatives to better know your beloved as well as their family and social environments, as Christians, we do the same by forming friendships and relationships with members of God's family. As in any family, some church members will be warm and accepting and serve as family "pillars" in church leadership roles. Other attendees will be standoffish and may have a personality type that is difficult to get to know. There may also be certain people in the pews who do not display the fruits of the Spirit. Thankfully, they are in church to learn about God, and hopefully, one day accept Jesus as Lord.

Special church services like baptism, Communion, and holy day celebrations often strengthen Christian connections by bringing us closer to God. Even though we cannot see Him physically, we can feel Him spiritually, which contributes to forging strong bonds with the God we love and serve.

Frequent prayer, which is discussed in more depth below in the section on Communication, is another building block of intimacy with God. Divorce lawyers often cite a lack of communication as a reason why marriages fail. In fact, inadequate communication may be the source of significant misunderstandings and conflicts throughout the world. Every relationship needs the glue of communication to keep people connected and in harmony. Maintain frequent contact with God and share your innermost thoughts and needs. Superficial or repetitive prayers are hollow and empty, void of meaning, and do nothing to strengthen a personal relationship with our Creator.

COMMON INTERESTS

Good friends or family members usually share similar interests. They do not necessarily agree with everything a loved one does, but they can find common ground for sharing concerns, goals, and efforts that bring them closer together.

Similarly, Christian faith and spiritual growth lead to expanded interests that we can share with our heavenly Father. People with little faith wait for God to tap them on the shoulder with guidance or discipline. But those with strong faith seek God's presence continually in their lives to enjoy a comfortable relationship with Him. They commune about everyday problems and give thanks for God's daily blessings.

What are God's interests? The spiritual well-being of His human children. He offers salvation to all, and it is the believers' collective responsibility to share the Gospel with everyone who will listen. The Lord has compassion on the broken-hearted and the lost, and we are to minister to them and represent God's love for them here on earth. That is the primary goal that Christians share with God.

When you share common interests and compassionate concerns with someone you care about, that brings you closer to each other. Participating in the other person's ministries or supporting them, however, can help you to forge a powerful emotional bond. The section titled Service below will explore that element further. The way we can approach God in this life to build a relationship with Him is to seek to know his mind and to adopt the same mindset. We will never be equals with God, but we can learn to consider and respond to human nature God's way by learning His ways:

> For "who has known the mind of the LORD that he may instruct Him?" But we have the mind of Christ.
> (I Corinthians 2:16 NKJV)

When you get married, you put your spouse first and blend your lives increasingly as you grow closer by building on the foundation of what has already been established. Over time, the marital bond grows stronger. Anyone who claims to be a Christian will put God above all else and live to please Him accordingly.

SHARED ACTIVITIES

In an intimate relationship, you want to be with the other person as much as possible. Although duties like family responsibilities and earning a living must also be tended, you try to spend every spare moment with the most important person in your life. Are you doing that with God? Or is time spent with

Him more of an afterthought to be worked into your schedule when convenient?

People who care deeply about each other, whether united by blood or law, share meaningful activities that may include necessary tasks as well as leisurely relaxation. When planning a weekday or a weekend, the loved one is always included. Although the pair will not spend every moment together, they will decide what to do with the other person in mind, knowing that certain options might be offensive or concerning.

In the same way, even though believers cannot spend every moment in God's presence with prayer, church worship, or ministry, we should carefully choose other activities that will not offend God. In fact, everything we do should be God-honoring. This includes how we treat others, how we dress in public, and how we talk to people – especially those that annoy us. Literally, everything we do should reflect the highest level of a personal relationship with our heavenly Father.

How is your driving? If you frequently speed and get traffic tickets, you are breaking the law. What does God's word say about that?

> *Let every soul be subject to the governing authorities. For there is no authority except from God, and the authorities that exist are appointed by God.*
> (Romans 13:1 NKJV)

Ladies, do you dress provocatively?

*...in like manner also, that the women adorn themselves
in modest apparel, with propriety and moderation, not
with braided hair or gold or pearls or costly clothing...*
(I Timothy 2:9 NKJV)

Are you spending time around sinful influences?

*Blessed is the man
Who walks not in the counsel of the [a]ungodly,
Nor stands in the path of sinners,
Nor sits in the seat of the scornful...*
(Psalms 1:1 NKJV)

Whatever your conduct at work and your demeanor around others, it should reflect a holy image of God so that everyone can see the relationship you cherish with the King of the universe:

*Therefore you shall be perfect, just as your Father in heaven
is perfect.*
(Matthew 5:48 NKJV)

Jesus does not seem to be saying in this passage that His followers will automatically live perfect lives. Instead, He appears to urge believers to strive for perfection as a reflection of our heavenly Father. This takes time. But every strong relationship is built by people who uphold each other and become like each other in meaningful ways.

And whatever you do, do it heartily, as to the Lord and not to men...

(Colossians 3:23 NKJV)

Make God an essential part of each day and every decision you make. When you want to be close to someone, you share every part of your life with that person. Choose your activities wisely, and let God lead.

MEANINGFUL COMMUNICATION

Everyday conversations with familiar people sound much the same.

"Hi, how are you?"

"Great, how about you?"

"Fine, thanks."

Even when conversations go more in-depth, they are often limited in scope. For example, you might ask a coworker how his son's school football team is doing this year, and you will probably get a predictable answer with occasional changes in details.

But when someone you care about wants to discuss politics, religion, or world affairs, you might get involved in more in-depth exchanges that enhance your understanding and appreciation of each other. Even when you disagree, friendly debates are often revealing and helpful in acknowledging more than one perspective on an issue. In most cases, your relationship with that person will grow deeper and become more prosperous.

How do you establish meaningful communication with God? As you would with a human who is important to you, take steps to commune in genuine and caring ways.

LISTEN.

Before trying to make yourself heard, be willing to hear what God has to say.

> *A wise man will hear and increase learning, And a man of understanding will attain wise counsel…*
> (Proverbs 1:5 NKJV)

It can be hard to stay quiet and listen to someone else speak. Sometimes you must wait until the person is ready to speak. But the Bible points out that wise people do just that – listen, hear, and learn.

You can listen for God's voice in many ways: Reading Scripture, listening to sermons, and meditating on God's presence in your life. He may speak to your spirit in a way that is difficult to describe in human terms. Find out what God is saying to you before trying to communicate with Him.

UNDERSTAND.

Some people give up reading the Bible because they cannot understand it: "The language is too old" or "Its principles are out of date." If you do not understand the Bible, then learn how to read it and study it for meaning. Sunday school class, online or campus courses, and Bible study groups can all help you learn how to understand the Bible's teachings. You can also use a study Bible and read commentaries that explain passages in detail.

BE HONEST.

Do not tell God in prayers just the things you think He wants to hear. Be honest about what troubles you. Speak up about things you do not understand. Apologize for wrongdoing. Humbly ask His forgiveness. Seek guidance and direction. God is the Lord over every aspect of your life. Acknowledge that by speaking with Him openly and sincerely in frequent prayer.

If you are not having daily conversations with God and opening your heart completely to Him, you cannot sustain an intimate relationship.

COMMITMENT

Relationship commitments seem to be fading fast in today's culture. Many people start and finish new relationships every couple of months. These relationships cannot last because the people involved invest so little of themselves into making them work. Following the infatuation phase, they settle into a honeymoon phase (often without marriage) and expect everything to go smoothly.

Without commitment and occasional hard work, most relationships are doomed to failure. People are changeable. We are also selfish. Expecting things to go our way from the get-go, we grow annoyed, frustrated, and angry before giving up and walking out. Time after time, people go through the same process, always finding disillusionment and failure. Couples break up, and families break down with little hope of restoration.

But a relationship with God is different. God never changes, and He puts great effort into establishing relationships with His children. He never gives up; we are the ones who walk away when the relationship does not progress the way we think it should. But God patiently waits for us to acknowledge our errors and return to Him, as he is always ready to forgive and accept his lost sheep.

What do you expect of God? Has He responded accordingly?

If not, have you given up on Him? Because He will never give up on you. Seek Him while He may be found:

But from there you will seek the LORD your God, and you will find Him if you seek Him with all your heart and with all your soul.
                                    (Deuteronomy 4:29 NKJV)

Stay committed to your relationship with God. That is the only way to enjoy real intimacy and make it last.

One night a fifty-year-old homeless man stood at the door of a city shelter.

"Come in," the doorkeeper said, letting him in.

Over a hot meal and coffee, one of the workers came over and sat down at Henry's table. "Did you get enough to eat? There's more at the serving table."

"This is plenty," Henry said. "Thank you. I'm grateful."

"Have you been here before?" the middle-aged man asked kindly.

Henry grinned after wiping his chin with the napkin. "I used to run a place like this. We had a shelter and gave out food and meals to the homeless." He chuckled before adding, "Then the tables turned, and I became one of them."

The worker nodded. "It can happen to anyone."

Sensing the man's empathy, Henry explained, "I used to be close to God. I talked to Him every morning and every evening. I was in church twice a week, and I read my Bible faithfully." He paused. "But a few years ago, my wife left me for another man. The kids were grown by then. Seemed like no one cared, so I stopped caring. And this is where I ended up."

He shook his head in frustration.

The other man listened thoughtfully. "You could come back," he suggested.

"To church?" Henry asked.

"To God. Reconnect with Him. He has a plan for you, and your life will change for the better."

Henry thought a moment and said, "You're right. God and I broke up before my wife and I did. I've got to get right with Him again before anything else can get better."

Staying committed to God is a guarantee for your future. God will meet your needs and guide you to where you are supposed to be, so you will never indeed be homeless again.

SERVICE

Working together toward a common goal establishes a valuable bond. As we overcome obstacles and achieve success, we realize that teamwork can do more than individualism. When you work in tandem with God's plan – using the skills and gifts He has bestowed on you – you will be your happiest and most fulfilled. Moreover, your actions will be pleasing to Him.

> ...clearly you are an epistle of Christ, ministered by us, written not with ink but by the Spirit of the living God,

*not on tablets of stone but on tablets of flesh, that is, of the
heart.*

(II Corinthians 3:3 NKJV)

God has a plan for your life and a purpose to be fulfilled.
He calls us to serve his Will in sharing the Gospel as well as
other acts of service according to each person's talents and gifts:

*Even so you, since you are zealous for spiritual gifts, let it
be for the edification of the church that you seek to excel.*
(I Corinthians 14:12 NKJV)

Christian author Dr. Gary Chapman wrote a book titled
The 5 Love Languages. One of the five main ways to express
love is through "acts of service." When we serve God by doing
whatever He calls us to do or equips us for, we honor Him with
love that bears witness to our intimate relationship with Him.
Not only will obedient service utilize your spiritual gifts and
serve God, but it will also testify to others of a close relationship with our heavenly Father.

World cultures today do little to promote pure and intimate relationships, and many have abandoned the principles
of marriage and monogamy. But intimacy is God's plan for
His family of believers. Starting with Adam and Eve in the
Garden of Eden in a private, natural setting, God has made
efforts down through history to interact with His chosen loved
ones in significant ways. In today's confused and critical culture, God continues to do His part; now, will you do yours?

Chapter
6

A Witness for the Lord

A true witness delivers souls, but a deceitful witness speaks lies.

(Proverbs 14:25 NKJV)

Despite criticizing and judging public figures before evidence is presented and a judicial process is initiated, our culture claims to value the clarifying nature of witness testimony in a legal court trial. Witnesses are one of the many kinds of evidence collected to support a legal claim or mount a defense. If you have ever been called as a witness in a court proceeding, it is because your testimony is sought due to the fact you are an expert in a critical aspect of the case, and you are acknowledged as someone truthful, reliable, and credible. Similarly, the best Christian witnesses are those who demonstrate the same qualities, especially in a culture that is skeptical and critical of Christianity. We must faithfully testify of God's Word:

For the word of the LORD is right, and all His work is done in truth.

(Psalms 33:4 NKJV)

As a bonafide witness for court or for Christ, it is vital to prepare beforehand. No serious witness walks into court without carefully selecting and reviewing the information that will be needed. A witness that expects to adlib about his or her background or knowledge is unlikely to make a good impression. An organized, reasonable, and understandable testimony can do much to influence those that hear it.

In the same way, anyone who wants to share a personal experience of salvation and a relationship with God as a Christian should prepare in advance before attempting to witness to unbelievers. Although a spontaneous conversation or an unplanned dispute can provide an opportunity to share convincing Biblical proofs of God and Jesus, you can feel more confident if you first plan your approach to sharing the Gospel message and take appropriate steps to prepare for your interactions with friends, relatives, coworkers, neighbors, or even strangers.

STUDY THE BIBLE

Start by reading the Bible – daily, or as frequently as you can. Scheduling consistency can be achieved when you read at the same time of day, like morning or evening, when you have uninterrupted time to read and meditate. Some people choose a special place for their "quiet time" with God. It might be a home office or a study area that is exclusively your domain. If you share space with others, designate a time when you will have that space to yourself. Pick a comfortable seat and maybe have a cup of coffee or tea on hand. As you settle into a routine, Bible study will become natural and enjoyable. You will look forward to it, and you will be disappointed if you miss a day due to illness or another commitment.

Choose a Bible translation that seems most natural to you in a version that is easily understood. A study Bible often includes scholarly notes, cross-references with related Scriptures, definitions of archaic terms and practices, Book outlines, and maps of Israel and Europe at different reference points in Scripture. This multifaceted approach to understanding the Bible can make it easier and more meaningful so that you will look forward to your time with God rather than find reasons to avoid it. Instead of self-imposed mandatory or superficial readings, you will continue to learn many interesting things during each day's reading.

Start with a chapter a day and increase your reading time as your schedule permits. Do not rush the process, or you might miss in-depth insights. Many Christians follow a schedule to read the Bible in a year, but just read at your own pace, so it does not become burdensome or meaningless. The goal can be to become familiar with God's Word by carefully and thoughtfully reading each book's chapter, no matter how long it takes.

The more you read and reread the Bible, the more you will see how all the Books fit together, from Genesis to Revelation. Both the Old Testament and the New Testament reveal God's plan for humanity from the creation of the world to the conclusion of earthly existence as we now know it. The Bible is God's revealed, archived communication to us through his prophets and the Apostles, with their writing covering about 4,000 years of history. Every Book of the Bible is God-inspired for a purpose:

All Scripture is given by inspiration of God, and is profitable for doctrine, for reproof, for correction, for instruction in righteousness...

(2 Timothy 3:16 NKJV)

An effective witness studies the context of a situation before finding the role they must play in analyzing and presenting essential information. In the same way, Christians must get to know the Bible thoroughly to understand God's entire plan for us and the roles that we have been given to share this information with others.

When you witness to someone about your Christian faith, there is a good chance that a person will ask questions about various parts of the Bible. You should be prepared to answer those questions to the best of your ability and point to specific Bible references that may help the listener to grasp the overarching message of salvation. Otherwise, your credibility as a witness will be weakened, and your listener may remain unconvinced of God's existence or purpose.

MEMORIZE KEY PASSAGES

It is not enough to read through the Bible completely several times, although that is an excellent starting place for laying a foundation of understanding in your mind to share with others. You also need to memorize important Scripture verses and passages that explain the salvation message. Many verses are easy to learn and can be recited as needed:

> *For God so loved the world that He gave His only begotten Son, that whoever believes in Him should not perish but have everlasting life.*
>
> (John 3:16 NKJV)

This beautiful verse reveals, in a single sentence, God's plan of redemption as presented through the ministry, death, and resurrection of Jesus Christ. If the person you are witnessing to has questions, they can be addressed with more verses like the following:

> *Jesus said to him, "I am the way, the truth, and the life. No one comes to the Father except through Me."*
>
> (John 14:6 NKJV)

A verse from the Apostle Paul's letter to the Romans further clarifies the Gospel message:

> *for all have sinned and fall short of the glory of God...*
>
> (Romans 3:23 NKJV)

No one can argue with the fact that everyone sins at times. We are imperfect, underserving to stand in our holy God's presence. But God has removed the barrier between our sinfulness and his purity by providing a unique plan of redemption and salvation for everyone who chooses to accept it:

> ...*that if you confess with your mouth the Lord Jesus and believe in your heart that God has raised Him from the dead, you will be saved.*
>
> (Romans 10:9 NKJV)

Memorizing Scriptures as these prepare you to speak with confidence about God's message to every person you meet. How they respond is up to them – with eternal consequences.

JOIN A CHURCH

In recent years, church membership and attendance have declined, paralleling the reduced number of Americans who claim to belong to a specific Christian denomination or affiliation. On October 17, 2019, the Pew Research Center published the following as part of its report on the decline of Christianity:

> The data shows that just like rates of religious affiliation, rates of religious attendance are declining.[3] Over the last decade, the share of Americans who say they attend religious services at least once or twice a month dropped by 7 percentage points, while the share who say they attend religious services less often (if at all) has risen by the same degree. In 2009, regular worship

attendees (those who attend religious services at least once or twice a month) outnumbered those who attend services only occasionally or not at all by a 52%-to-47% margin. Today those figures are reversed; more Americans now say they attend religious services a few times a year or less (54%) than say they attend at least monthly (45%).

(accessed August 29, 2020, https://www.pewforum.org/2019/10/17/in-u-s-decline-of-christianity-continues-at-rapid-pace/)

More than ever, in our nation's history, Christians need to join a church to strengthen its ranks and find congregational and pastoral support for faith and life in Christ. Also, church services and congregational activities provide an essential network of information and inspiration that help to prepare believers to share their testimony of Christian faith. Sunday school classes, pastoral sermons, and Bible fellowships and church social activities can strengthen members' beliefs and provide encouragement and examples for witnessing outreach.

Trying to witness as a loner without a church affiliation may not be productive. Jesus sent out His disciples in pairs rather than as individuals. He taught that when conflicts arise between believers, it should be resolved privately and individually, but if needed, by taking along a witness or two:

> [15] *"Moreover if your brother sins against you, go and tell him his fault between you and him alone. If he hears you, you have gained your brother. [16] But if he will not hear, take with you one or two more, that 'by the mouth of two or three witnesses every word may be established.'"*
>
> (Matthew 18:15-16 NKJV)

The End Times prophecies include a reference to Two Witnesses who play a key role. Synergy through two or more persons can be a more potent force for good than individual testimony:

> *Though one may be overpowered by another, two can withstand him. And a threefold cord is not quickly broken.*
>
> (Ecclesiastes 4:12 NKJV)

Be open to learning from your church family. Be willing to share your witness to unbelievers as part of a Christian team. As an active church member, you can also contribute to important ministries while learning from peers and mentors. Their wisdom, imparted to you, adds to your knowledge base that can be offered as part of your witness testimony to unbelievers.

LISTEN TO SERMONS

Effective listening in the church is more than staying awake during the sermon. It means carefully hearing the pastor's message and pondering his words. There may be a sermon outline to follow along with or Bible passages for reference. Listen to what the preacher is saying, and be sure you understand the meaning.

If you do not, ask about it when you can so that the message can be put to good use and bear fruit when added to your testimony.

Look for the context of the sermon. What is the theme, and what are the main points the sermon is making? Could you replicate a mini version of the sermon if someone asked you to? Would you be able to interpret the key ideas so that they could be easily grasped by someone who does not know much about God or the Bible?

If you cannot get to church to hear the service live, download the audio recordings. Listen more than once for added meaning and future reference. Take notes about the main topics and takeaway lessons. Research shows that writing about what you are listening to helps to reinforce the message and enables you to retain it longer and in greater detail.

Find more sermons online by speakers who are in sync with your pastor, your denomination, or the Bible as the inspired Word of God. You might be introduced to new perspectives to a particular Bible passage that will enhance your comprehension of and appreciation for it and the Gospel overall. This additional perspective could come in handy if at some point you witness to someone from a different background who is not fully following your testimony drawn from your personal church sermons. If the messages are based on the Biblical version of the Gospel message without adding anything to it or detracting from it, you should be able to safely adapt parts of the message for witnessing purposes.

Sermons, Sunday school lessons, and small group discussions will increase your understanding of Bible teachings. They can also add to your preparation as an effective witness to reach the unsaved.

Consult Additional Resources

Not everyone can add a Bible class to their busy schedules. But if you can take an online course or register for a workshop or a seminar, you can expand your Biblical understanding. You may be able to enroll in a class that focuses on witness ministry or refining your testimony. Professionals and experts can help you prepare an approach and introduction to someone you want to share the Gospel with.

There are plenty of books and videos that can be reviewed at your leisure. Among them are classic works like Josh McDowell's *Evidence that Demands a Verdict* (and his related works). Ravi Zacharias, a world-renowned Christian apologist, has published books like *Beyond Opinion* that may be useful. Tony Evans' book *Can God Be Trusted in Trials?* is especially helpful in ministering to people who are struggling with life's difficulties and who feel unsure about establishing a relationship with God. Many fine Christian authors specialize in topics that serve as excellent witnessing tools. Browse online bookstores or ask your pastor for recommendations of resources that can serve as useful testimony tools.

GET INVOLVED IN MINISTRY

Participating in church outreach programs that minister to the unsaved can be a practical training ground as you prepare to become a witness for God. You can start by listening to how experienced church members or ministry volunteers witness to others. You will be able to decide which strategies you feel comfortable with and those you probably will not use.

Within the group, you may be given opportunities to witness to new members or perhaps to give your testimony at church. These activities enable you to share your conversion story and respond to questions and feedback from listeners. Some will be very supportive. Others may have questions about your experience that will further refine your presentation and be more prepared in the future.

With experience and support and defining your role in ministry, you may be able to talk informally with clients you work with and share your personal story of salvation. This might at first be offered casually in conversation. Later, as you develop confidence and work with more individuals or larger groups, your testimony may become more organized and polished. It should not sound too formal to avoid sounding pretentious or talking at a level that some listeners might not understand. Keep it simple and sincere, and many people will respond in kind.

ADJUST YOUR ATTITUDE

While maintaining a positive outlook, be careful not to look down on those struggling with overtly sinful behaviors, like substance abuse or fornication. Called to love the sinner but hate the sin, we should be respectful when telling others about our salvation and sharing hope with those who desperately need to hear this message. Many are seeking it, but others are not. All deserve the same opportunity offered courteously, whatever their response.

> *For the Son of Man has come to save that which was lost.*
> (Matthew 18:11 NKJV)

Remember, we are all sinners; all have sinned and fall short of God's glory. It is only through the blood of Jesus and his death on the cross that we can enter God's presence with prayer and thanksgiving. Only through Jesus's resurrection can we look forward to spending eternity with God. "There, but for the grace of God, go I…" is a well-known reminder.

We should remain teachable and correctible if we get something wrong. We should also be kindhearted and caring toward those who earnestly want to know more about God. Even if someone does not accept Jesus as Savior in response to your witness, if they have heard your words, you have planted a seed, and it may be up to another believer to water the soil while still, a third Christian will harvest the fruit of your seed's planting.

PRAY FAITHFULLY

*And He said to them, "Go into all the world and preach
the gospel to every creature."*

(Mark 16:15 NKJV)

As you seek to become an effective witness for the Lord,
trust him to lead. Pray daily and faithfully, making all your
needs known to God. He has a plan for your life, and it will be
revealed in His timing.

Ask God to bring the people into your purview to whom
He wishes you to testify about his love and grace. Ask Him to
give you the right time and the right words. Also, ask for the
right attitude to accept whatever outcome ensues from your
witnessing efforts. Do not be discouraged if the encounter with
an unbeliever does not end with a faith commitment, but continue praying about that person and leave the outcome to God:

*The effective, fervent prayer of a righteous man avails
much.*

(James 5:16[b] NKJV)

Someday, Jesus will judge each of us from His Judgment
Seat, one judgment for the saved and another for the unsaved.
Your earthly deeds will be reviewed and evaluated. Make your
witnessing outreach as strong as it can be by considering the
above steps. You might only have one chance to talk to an individual who needs to hear the Gospel, so prepare now for the
opportunity of a lifetime – or an eternity.

God is faithful in this faithless world. The culture does not care about God or Christians. They do not view sin as God views it. Learn all you can about God and His plan for judgment when that day comes. Prepare your witness to align with God's Word so that you will be ready with answers for anyone that God brings into your life.

Sheree Taylor often felt guilty for not sharing her faith publicly. Sometimes in casual conversations, a question about God would come up. Sheree would answer politely without saying much because she was shy and unsure of how to answer people's questions. One Sunday morning, as Sheree returned from church, her next-door neighbor Mrs. Williams was sweeping her front porch and waved.

"Good morning! How was church?" Mrs. Williams knew Sheree went to church, but they had never discussed it in detail, and Sheree had not yet invited her neighbor to come with her.

Sheree had just gotten out of her car in the driveway and called back, "Um, it was nice." She wanted to say more because Mrs. Williams did not seem to be a Christian believer, but Sheree wasn't sure what to add.

Mrs. Williams asked, "What did your pastor preach on?"

Sheree stood there awkwardly before turning to her own porch. "It was about being ready to share our faith, similar to a witness in court."

Shaking her head, the neighbor said, "Sounds legalistic. That's the problem with churches and religion today, too many rules."

Sheree smiled apologetically, again wishing she could say something to make a positive impact on Mrs. Williams, but she couldn't think of anything. "It's not that bad."

"Well, you have a nice day," Mrs. Williams said as she turned and went into her house.

Sheree wished she could have been a better witness about her faith. If she had been more familiar with the Bible and had seen examples of witnessing from church friends, she could have been ready to extend the conversation with her neighbor. Now Sheree realized she had better prepare for the next conversation, hoping the opportunity would soon arise.

Twenty-first-century culture is full of naysayers who claim God is dead or church is meaningless. Christians must be ready to share the truth as witnesses of the faith through the Gospel message revealed in Jesus's words, ministry, death, and resurrection.

One day before the judgment seat, Jesus will testify about your salvation. Will you now testify of His saving power to those who are otherwise doomed to hell?

Chapter 7

Maintaining Victory

But thanks be to God, who gives us the victory through our
Lord Jesus Christ.

(I Corinthians 15:57 NKJV)

Culture wars are being waged all around us, not only in the US, but around the world. Even conservative non-Christians are taking a stand against the immoral, degenerate movements that make society a battleground. Issues like abortion, euthanasia, non-binary gender identities, and legalization of drugs are high-profile conflicts that force Christians to choose whether to stand for their beliefs or give in to public pressure.

Passion versus reason has always been a primary struggle of humanity. For Christians, it began in the Garden of Eden when Adam and Eve were presented with the choice of obeying God or giving in to secular persuasion. This dichotomy of good versus evil and God versus secularism has continued down through history to the twenty-first century with no sign of slowing.

Fortunately, our human conscience continues to work despite Satan's efforts to muffle it with temptation and rewards offered by society or doubts sown about faith. Like the wise woman of Proverbs, the voice of reason continues to cry out to those who will listen:

> *For wisdom is better than rubies, And all the things one may desire cannot be compared with her.*
> (Proverbs 8:11 NKJV)

Christians who love God and want to avoid sin will seek wisdom and flee the harlotry of godless society:

> *Thus they were defiled by their own works, and played the harlot by their own deeds.*
> (Psalm 106:39 NKJV)

In this context, the word "harlot" refers to turning away from God and seeking the pleasures of this world. You may know people who run after fame, wealth, success, or other pleasures that have little to do with God or His plan for their lives. But God gives each of us a choice so that we may pursue worldly desires or choose Jesus as our Lord and Savior. The choice is sharply divided with opposite outcomes: secularism focuses on the here and now of pleasures to be gained in a material world while Godliness leads to a life led in pursuit of knowing God and pleasing Him with our conduct according to the Bible's principles.

PUT GOD FIRST

There is nothing in the Bible that says you cannot earn a decent living or become wealthy.

> *That I may cause those who love me to inherit wealth,*
> *That I may fill their treasuries.*
> (Proverbs 8:21 NKJV)

Many such Scriptures can be found in the Bible that apply to God's people. However, notice the description of wealth: those "who love me" can "inherit wealth." First, we must love God and devote our lives to serving Him. As we use our God-given gifts to bring Him glory and help others to find Him, He can reward us accordingly if that is part of His plan for our life. The word "inherit" used in this verse might not just mean to receive family wealth passed down as an inheritance. It could mean that receiving wealth is an inheritance from God Himself to those who love and honor Him.

But wealth may also be more of a means to an end. As indicated in Jesus's parable of the three talents, the one who gained the most return on his talent multiplied not only the original investment but also was the person of the three who received even more when the master returned to reward the workers accordingly. Jesus seems to be telling us that whatever goods we receive from God – wealth, health, skills, or opportunities – we should use them to serve God. In the Old Testament, when one of the Israelites stole plunder that was not to be touched, he and his family were publicly executed by stoning:

> *Then Joshua, and all Israel with him, took Achan the son of Zerah, the silver, the garment, the wedge of gold, his sons, his daughters, his oxen, his donkeys, his sheep, his tent, and all that he had, and they brought them to the Valley of Achor.*
>
> (Joshua 7:24 NKJV)

Money, investments, and valuable possessions are gifts from God that arrive in His timing. Trying to get ahead of God's plan by playing the lottery or cheating on your taxes violates God's laws. When we put to good use the bounty that God has given us, the return on our investment can be vast and earn even more generous gifts and rewards.

Seeking a luxurious lifestyle, fame, or status as your life's primary goal is incompatible with Biblical principles.

> *"No one can serve two masters; for either he will hate the one and love the other, or else he will be loyal to the one and despise the other. You cannot serve God and mammon…"*
>
> (Matthew 6:24 NKJV)

Even if you are trying to work overtime and extra shifts to bank more income and build your savings, be careful that it does not infringe on your spiritual responsibilities. Do not put the love of money ahead of everything else, as it often leads to trouble in all areas of life:

> *For the love of money is a root of all kinds of evil, for which some have strayed from the faith in their greediness, and pierced themselves through with many sorrows.*
> (I Timothy 6:10 NKJV)

Attorneys report that money is one of the leading causes of divorce. Some sayings about money are the more we have, the more we want. How much is enough? "Just a little bit more."

Again, it is not wrong to work hard, earn fair wages, build a nest egg, and be good at your job. But if these things disrupt your relationship with God or your family, then your priorities need to be adjusted.

The same principle applies to other areas of life where we strongly desire worldly things like "keeping up with the Joneses" or becoming prideful over possessions and accomplishments. Society encourages and rewards these behaviors, but God's Word teaches us to be humble and put others first.

Relationships are another major battleground for Satan and his demonic troops. A glance at today's leading news stories show families in turmoil, robbing and killing each other, with people changing partners or spouses whenever they get tired of the one they are with. Getting a divorce is almost as easy as selling a home or changing jobs. It does not seem to matter that lives are damaged, children are suffering, and people just keep getting emotionally injured and hardened with wounds that cannot heal. God has a clear plan for relationships and marriage. Unmarried people should treat each other with respect and refrain from sexual intimacy. Married people should remain devoted to each other until death takes one or both. While unusual circumstances may sometimes lead to other outcomes, God's original plan for families was clear and beneficial. Today, former spouses or partners are battle-scarred, and their descendants continue the legacy of swapping partners without hesitation or guilt.

Children are the most vulnerable victims, with the statistics increasing to show many kids are physically, sexually, or emotionally abused by the parents who are supposed to protect them. Some domestic violence experts claim that the home is the most dangerous place for children to be in our culture. Many adults have become so self-centered that everything and everyone must serve their interests and needs. Children who are unable to meet these needs are neglected, abused, or killed.

When we put God first and build a relationship with Him, everything else will fall into place. It might not happen immediately or smoothly, but God will make a way when there seems to be no way. Think about how different our culture would be if everyone turned to God, repented of their sins, accepted Jesus as Savior, and followed the Lord's teachings.

A July 6, 2017 article titled "Faith and Marriage: Better Together?" published by the Institute for Family Studies indicated that "Couples who attend religious services together are happier in their relationships than are their peers who don't regularly attend church" (https://ifstudies.org/blog/faith-and-marriage-better-together#:~:text=Religious%20communities%20can%20provide%20important%20resources%20for%20a,that%20the%20couple%20that%20attends%20together%2C%20stays%20together).

Of course, God has known this since he created humans. It was His plan for us to fellowship with Him as well as each other. Unfortunately, most people have lost interest in communing with their Creator, preferring to focus their time and attention on the glittery goods of this world. Hedonism rules the day, with substance addiction rates growing exponentially, suicide increasing, violence exploding, and hatefulness overflowing into every public channel affecting our lives. This may be the worst age in human history in which humanity has descended into depravity and base desires to demand that personal rights and freedoms be acknowledged and accepted by all, no matter how illogical, unsound, or dangerous these beliefs might be. Such is the culture we live in today as the Bible predicted 2,000 years ago:

> But know this, that in the last days [a]perilous times will come: ² For men will be lovers of themselves, lovers of money, boasters, proud, blasphemers, disobedient to parents, unthankful, unholy, unloving, [b]unforgiving, slanderers, without self-control, brutal, despisers of good, traitors, headstrong, haughty, lovers of pleasure rather than lovers of God, having a form of godliness but denying its

power. And from such people turn away!
(2 Timothy 3:1-5 NKJV)

Satan has been waging war against humans since his fall from Heaven. But we know, as Christians, that the battle for salvation has been fought and won by Jesus on the cross and His resurrection from the grave. Those who accept his atoning punishment in our place for the sins we have committed are saved from eternal damnation. But to achieve victories over daily skirmishes fostered by a brutal society, we need the protective armor of God and rely on his strength, not ours. We can, however, do our part in fleeing temptation and keeping our feet on the path that leads to sanctification when we finally meet God face to face.

SEEK GOD'S PROVISION AND PROTECTION

Even victorious warriors must be watchful against the wiles of the enemy who may trick them into believing themselves successful before experiencing a blind attack from behind. Christians can never let their guard down even with – or especially after – social victories in battles with worldly and demonic forces.

> *For we do not wrestle against flesh and blood, but against principalities, against powers, against the rulers of the darkness of this age, against spiritual hosts of wickedness in the heavenly places.*
>
> (Ephesians 6:12 NKJV)

This world is not our eternal home. We are strangers passing through, trying to light the path to Jesus for others struggling in spiritual darkness. But we must be careful to avoid traps set by the enemy and escape being pulled into useless debates about ungodly issues that serve no Biblical purpose. There is a time to stand up and be heard as God's ambassador here on earth. But choose your battles carefully. Try to ensure that your listeners are ready to hear your message of salvation. Do not be lured into a false trap of accepting what appears to be a logical defense of unbridled behavior that the Bible expressly calls sin.

Maintain your victory march without looking left or right to consider the evil snares society puts in your path. Many Christians have been caught in such traps, sometimes with devastating outcomes. Keep your eyes on Jesus and trust in His power to guide you.

More than ever, it is crucial to stay connected to your church. You must regularly attend, and you should volunteer where needed. Invite unsaved neighbors and friends to go with you. Pay attention to the sermons and get involved with Sunday school as well as a group Bible study. Take your children to church and discuss the messages with them afterward. Being part of a church family is not just an enjoyable social activity. It is a safe refuge from the world's deceptions. But be sure your church's doctrine is grounded in God's Word. If you hear false teachings, ask the pastor about them to be sure you understood correctly. When it is confirmed that the church has abandoned solid Biblical doctrine, leave and find another church home based on Scriptural truth. Beware of wolves in sheep's clothing – false shepherds who are eager to lead the unsuspecting believers away from the truth to justify their distortion of it:

> *Now the Spirit expressly says that in latter times some will depart from the faith, giving heed to deceiving spirits and doctrines of demons…*
>
> (1 Timothy 4:1 NKJV)

Become even more rooted in Bible reading and meditating on the Word. You cannot evaluate a church doctrine or a pastor's preaching until you know for yourself what the Bible says and means. God instituted the Christian church when the risen Jesus gave His disciple Peter the keys of the kingdom:

> *And I also say to you that you are Peter, and on this rock I will build My church, and the gates of Hades shall not prevail against it.*
>
> (Matthew 16:18 NKJV)

Believers must remain unified if we are to maintain victory. There is safety in numbers. We cannot let down our guard for a single day or allow ourselves to be separated from our Christian faith and saved friends. If you find yourself struggling spiritually to hold on to faith, to flee temptation, or to obey God, call your pastor or one of the church elders. When you find yourself struggling in certain areas of life, contact your ministry leaders, or get in touch with a Christian friend. Pray earnestly to God for His provision and protection. God has provided these resources to you as a member of his Church and the family of God.

When seventeen-year-old Jeremy accepted Jesus as his Savior at a church revival, he was ecstatic. "I'm saved – I'm going to Heaven! Satan will never get me!"

His last statement was only partly true. As a confirmed believer in Jesus, Jeremy was destined for an eternity spent in Heaven with God. Nothing could change that. But Satan could – and would – continue to tempt Jeremy to commit sins that the teenager knew were wrong. In one way, Jeremy took his salvation for granted, believing "once saved, always saved" so that nothing he would ever do wrong could separate him from God's love. But Satan tries to disable Christians if he cannot prevent their salvation. He will try everything to make believers miserable and ineffective in maintaining a Christian lifestyle to thwart their influence over others.

When people around him saw the change in Jeremy after his baptism, many, like his grandparents and single dad, who was raising the boy, celebrated with him. Others, like his mother, who had abandoned the family years before, sneered at his faith. "You're no better than the rest of us," she posted on social media, "so stop being a hypocrite." His friends also laughed at Jeremy or started avoiding him, not wanting to hear his praise of the Bible and love for God. Jeremy had never felt so alone

– which was precisely where Satan wanted him.

A new girl transferred to Jeremy's high school and immediately sought his friendship. Then she began flirting with him, and due to loneliness, Jeremy gave in to her romantic advances. Two months later, the girl revealed she was pregnant, sending Jeremy into a panic. What would people think of his faith now? How could he raise a child? Should he and the baby's mother get married or place the child for adoption? Jeremy did not lose his faith, but his life changed dramatically because he fell for Satan's wiles. It will take time for the teen to figure out the next steps in his life. His testimony will be put on hold for a long time, and Jeremy is learning a hard lesson about maintaining victory in faith while keeping watch against worldly temptations. Fortunately, he has a support system in his father and church friends, so he will have help in making God-honoring decisions if he sticks to that path.

When the culture calls out to you like the adulteress in Proverbs, do not listen. Turn to your Christian church home and family instead:

> How the faithful city has become a harlot! It was full of justice; righteousness lodged in it, but now murderers.
> (Isaiah 1:21 NKJV)

In the twenty-first century, everyone in this world has become corrupt and defiled:

All we like sheep have gone astray; we have turned, every one, to his own way; and the LORD has laid on Him the iniquity of us all.

(Isaiah 53:6 NKJV)

God offers hope in having sent Jesus to take our punishment. The battle is won – victory is ours!

But the world at large does not recognize or celebrate our triumph. Neither does Satan. They make war against believers, so you must be ready to continue fighting for faith by putting on the armor of God:

Finally, my brethren, be strong in the Lord and in the power of His might. Put on the whole armor of God, that you may be able to stand against the wiles of the devil. For we do not wrestle against flesh and blood, but against principalities, against powers, against the rulers of the darkness of this age, against spiritual hosts of wickedness in the heavenly places. ...

(Ephesians 6:10-18 NKJV)

Rejoice! We are victorious in the Lord!

But there is more to do before we can claim the total defeat of the Enemy. Be prepared for the evil in this world to try you, test you, and trick you:

If you were of the world, the world would love its own. Yet because you are not of the world, but I chose you out of the world, therefore the world hates you.

(John 15:19 NKJV)

God is leading the charge. We must do our part and fall in rank as He leads the way to complete and permanent Victory! The Battle of Armageddon will come – but we already know the outcome, and we are on the winning side!

Chapter
8

A Walk of Love

And now abide faith, hope, love, these three; but the greatest of these is love.

(I Corinthians 13:13 NKJV)

During his earthly ministry, Jesus had much to say about love, including God's love for him, as well as God's love for us. That is why God sent Jesus to die in our place as atonement for sin:

For God so loved the world that He gave His only begotten Son, that whoever believes in Him should not perish but have everlasting life. –

(John 3:16 NKJV)

Many traditional church hymns and contemporary songs emphasize God's love for the humans he created and his desire for them all to be saved. Yet, we are given a choice of living for God or loving this world. Sadly, most people choose this world. Eventually, they will pay a heavy price for clinging to sin instead of accepting salvation.

In this book, we have been examining how Christianity is juxtaposed against secular culture. Everyone gets to choose the way they want to live, and each of us will be judged for that choice. Either we will be rewarded by spending eternity with our holy God, or we will be doomed to a fiery hell in the company of Satan and his demons. The choice should be clear-cut and easy, but for many, it is not. They are enticed by worldly pleasures to reject the spiritual joy offered by God.

God created humans for fellowship. He provided a perfect environment and a pain-free existence. But that was not enough for Adam and Eve. They listened to the serpent and bought into His lies that they could become equal to God, having their cake and eating it, too, except their temptation was the forbidden fruit.

Despite their disobedience and resulting punishment, God continued to love His human children. Through generation after generation, He provided prophets, judges, and kings to guide His chosen people to their rightful inheritance in the Promised Land. He offered them an exclusive relationship to be his people with Him as their God through leaders like Moses and King David. But the people continued to stray from God's principles and their promises of obedience. Time and again, God disciplined them through wars and captivity, sometimes plague as well. Although the chosen people repented, they did not remain faithful for long. Such has been the age-old relationship between God and people since the first couple in the Garden of Eden. God continues to love us and has made atonement for us. But we, like sheep, continue to go astray, leaving a trail of pain, loss, and despair until we repent and reunite with our heavenly Father. The relationship with God has been often one-sided, with God doing most of the work to provide protection, guidance, and love.

Love is the dominant theme throughout the Bible, and the Bible is God's love letter to us. God first loved us so that we might love Him in return. His Word teaches us how to love as described in the words of Paul's letter to the church at Corinth:

> *Love suffers long and is kind; love does not envy; love does not parade itself, is not puffed up; does not behave rudely, does not seek its own, is not provoked, thinks no evil; does not rejoice in iniquity, but rejoices in the truth; bears all things, believes all things, hopes all things, endures all things. Love never fails.*
>
> (I Corinthians 13:4-8 NKJV)

God lovingly leads His people. Christians ought to respond to others in the same way.

CULTURAL LOVE

Today's culture views love differently than God does. The cultural perspective on love is that everyone should love themselves first and do whatever it takes to maintain self-love while getting others to love us as well. For many people, this involves breaking the law or changing the laws to fit their interests. A majority do not claim to love God nor show it in their lives. They do not demonstrate Biblical principles in how they live or interact with others. The primary objective of modern life seems to be to get ahead at any cost, even if that means killing the unborn, the elderly, and the infirm. Some break laws with impunity, arguing against God-instituted authorities, hurting themselves and others by their actions.

Social definitions of love at present favor the needs of the individual over those of the family. Each person, it is argued, has the right to pursue happiness and love at almost any cost, disrupting families, and finances while doing so. Love appears to be arbitrary and transitory. No one is "obligated" to love parents or spouses; love is a vaporous emotion that comes and goes at will. You cannot predict it or hold on to it. You just let it take you wherever it wants to go.

New expressions of love violate God's boundaries and break traditional molds. In recent years, people have been known to marry pets, buildings, computers, the self, and close relatives. Some of these "unions" are symbolic rather than realistic in nature. Others follow conventional marriage services and practices to establish new forms of romantic coupling and family structures.

Alleged friends attack each other on social media. Parents

kill their children, and vice versa. Where is love in these traditional relationships? More importantly, where is God?

God is the same always; He never changes. It is we and our culture that have changed. Let us agree to return to God's plan for a loving society based on principles outlined in Scripture.

Committed Christians will honor and uphold God's view of love against the distorted configurations in today's culture.

LOVE GOD

Jesus said to him, "'You shall love the Lord your God with all your heart, with all your soul, and with all your mind.'"
(Matthew 22:37 NKJV)

Jesus taught us how to love God. We are to love Him with all our being – not holding back any part of ourselves. We cannot say we love God with our lips but think evil thoughts in our minds. We are not to go to church but then also go to places that are not sanctioned by God. Our emotions, our spiritual praise and prayers, and our thoughts and learning should all be dedicated to loving and serving God. If we are divided between God and the world, we cannot serve two masters. It will not work.

How do we love God? By serving others. Jesus explained that whatever we do to help the "least" of the people in need, it is as if we are doing the same for Jesus Himself. When we put others' needs ahead of our own, we are modeling humility and enacting service pleasing to God. We do not need to march around town boasting about our emotional love toward God. Simple actions with a humble attitude will speak loud and clear to anyone who is watching.

The love we demonstrate for others is born out of our love for God, even for those we consider as enemies. When we put God first and love Him with our whole being, He helps us to have the right attitude toward those that not only can help them understand God and perhaps come to know him, but also helps us to grow in faith and love for the Father.

> *Trust in the LORD with all your heart,*
> *And lean not on your own understanding;*
> *In all your ways acknowledge Him,*
> *And He shall [a]direct your paths.*
>
> (Proverbs 3:5, 6 NKJV)

God is ever-present and always hears your prayers. Put Him first and seek him first to make Him the focus of your life. When you love Him, you will feel His love even more as it blossoms in your life and extends to others.

> *"Therefore know that the LORD your God, He is God,*
> *the faithful God who keeps covenant and mercy for a*
> *thousand generations with those who love Him and keep*
> *His commandments..."*
>
> (Deuteronomy 7:9 NKJV)

Unlike the unsaved people of this world who can leave you without notice or care, God will always be faithful to His relationship with His loved ones. He will never abandon you. Feel His love when you pray, and give Him love in worship. God wants to speak to everyone who listens for His voice.

> *"And now, Israel, what does the LORD your God require of you, but to fear the LORD your God, to walk in all His ways and to love Him, to serve the LORD your God with all your heart and with all your soul..."*
> (Deuteronomy 10:12 NKJV)

LOVE YOUR FAMILY

The Bible outlines several guidelines to help us understand God's plan for family life. There are numerous examples of what we should do and should not do to have successful families. Love is the primary glue that holds a family together. Of course, love should be received from God and given back to Him before while sharing it with spouses and children and extended family members.

Contrary to God's will for humanity, people have increasingly become hostile to each other, even to those they should love the most. News reports abound of husbands and wives killing each other and destroying their children. Parents do not like to see their children quarreling and fighting, and God is no exception. Our heavenly father wants us to care for one another and be committed to each other within the sanctification of our marriage vows and family commitments.

Being human, our weaknesses often overcome us. We hurt the ones we love the most. If we are Christians who genuinely want to follow Jesus and serve God, then we repent of our shortcomings by asking God's forgiveness as well as apologizing to the people we hurt. We also make serious efforts to do better. Every night before bed, we should reflect on the day's actions and ask God to reveal our wrongdoings. By text, phone, email, or in person, we should make amends to the people we hurt and repair the relationship insofar as they will allow it. Letting conflicts and hurts drag on will only make it harder to set things right. Be honest and be humble in admitting your guilt and offering to make atonement. If more husbands and wives faithfully shouldered that responsibility, we would have fewer broken families and divorces. As part of a chain reaction or domino effect, there would be fewer cases of child abuse, less juvenile delinquency, reduced numbers of drug addicts and alcoholics, and possibly better-managed mental health. Crime rates might decline, with more families sticking together and protecting each other.

The Bible gives us numerous examples of relationships that went wrong when people stopped listening to God and obeying his laws. Abraham and Sarah, Jacob and his two wives, David and Bathsheba, and Solomon, with his harem along with Ahab and Jezebel, are striking examples of dysfunctional marriages and strife-filled families that warn us against indulging our passions and ignoring God in this sin-steeped world.

However, the Bible also provides lovely examples of harmonious marriages and well-adjusted families that put God first and love each other in uplifting ways: Boaz and Ruth, Joseph and Mary, and Aquila and Priscilla illustrate how God-honoring couples fulfill God's purpose in their lives and become beacons of faith to others.

The Apostle Paul's inspired letter to the early Christian church at Ephesus reveals God's intended roles for wives and husbands:

> *Wives, submit to your own husbands, as to the Lord. For the husband is head of the wife, as also Christ is head of the church; and He is the Savior of the body.*
> (Ephesians 5:22-23 NKJV)

Brief and straightforward, this passage indicates that men should lead their families, with women respecting and accepting their husbands' leadership as the head of the household. It confers enormous responsibility on husbands to be Christ-like in looking after their loved ones, similar to how Christ leads the church. Husbands must not wield power over their wives and children for selfish purposes, but rather lovingly guide them with the shared purpose of obeying God and glorifying him in their marriage and family.

The chapter of Ephesians 5 continues in a more significant

explanation about the husband's marital duties:

> *Husbands, love your wives, just as Christ also loved the church and gave Himself for her, that He might [g]sanctify and cleanse her with the washing of water by the word, that He might present her to Himself a glorious church, not having spot or wrinkle or any such thing, but that she should be holy and without blemish. So husbands ought to love their own wives as their own bodies; he who loves his wife loves himself. For no one ever hated his own flesh, but nourishes and cherishes it, just as the Lord does the church. For we are members of His body, [h]of His flesh and of His bones. "For this reason a man shall leave his father and mother and be joined to his wife, and the two shall become one flesh." This is a great mystery, but I speak concerning Christ and the church. Nevertheless, let each one of you in particular so love his own wife as himself, and let the wife see that she respects her husband.*
>
> (Ephesians 5:25-33 NKJV)

This clear passage lays out the husband's role and responsibility to his wife. It is lengthier and more descriptive than the previous verses and far longer than the guidelines provided for wives. Essentially, men are to love their wives as much as they love themselves – and be willing to sacrifice themselves if needed. Women should respect their husbands, which would preclude nagging, criticizing, and giving the "silent treatment." Husbands should be treated as well as, or better than, a wife would treat a male supervisor, colleague, or client.

Working on these relationships alone could fill most of our waking hours. But God enables us to honor his commands and to do even more: love other people as well as Him and our families.

LOVE OTHERS

You are probably thinking you have enough to worry about with organizing your spiritual life, your marriage and family life, and handling job duties without being concerned for other people. But God has assigned us that duty, and if we want to be loyal followers of Christ, we must accept all His teachings.

A new commandment I give to you, that you love one another; as I have loved you, that you also love one another. By this all will know that you are My disciples, if you have love for one another.

(John 13:34-35 NKJV)

This is a tall order! Jesus loved us so much that he was brutally beaten before an agonizing death on the cross as a common criminal. He left His perfect Father in heaven to live among the lowly here on earth. Although most people ignore Jesus's precious gift of salvation and eternal life, some do embrace it and live accordingly. But how many of us are willing to love others – unlovable people or those we do not know – in the same way? It seems impossible...until we ask God for the power to love others as He loves us.

The Apostle Paul writes with passion concerning our

response of love to others. The instructions we received are especially applicable today. Paul writes,

> *Be kindly affectionate to one another with brotherly love,*
> *in honor giving preference to one another...*
> (Romans 12:10 NKJV)

You might not feel warm emotional love toward someone you do not know. We must also remember Biblical love is not about feeling warm and fuzzy. Biblical love is all about treatment and actions. One way you may demonstrate love to others is by donating time or money to local charities and volunteering at a church ministry to reach others. If every believer contributed to helping others the way Jesus showed us, instead of criticizing secular people and movements that do not follow Biblical principles, the world might look at Christianity in a more positive light and be more open to receiving the Gospel.

LOVE YOURSELF

Finally, let us remember that the Holy Spirit indwells each Christian believer so that we must love ourselves in the sense of meeting our basic living needs and maintaining a holy existence:

> *...for the kingdom of God is not eating and drinking, but*
> *righteousness and peace and joy in the Holy Spirit.*
> (Romans 14:17 NKJV)

After accepting Jesus as Savior and being baptized, you are filled with the Holy Spirit, who will guide you and serve as your conscience if you are willing to heed His voice.

Jesus told us to love others as ourselves. He did not say we are not supposed to love ourselves, but rather, not love ourselves more than others or more than God. That means taking care of yourself. Stay healthy – physically, mentally, and spiritually. Enjoy the life that God has given you and avoid the lure of worldly pleasures that can damage your witness and torture your soul.

Or do you not know that your body is the temple of the Holy Spirit who is in you, whom you have from God, and you are not your own?
(I Corinthians 6:19 NKJV)

As believers, we are bought with a price and belong to the Lord. His Spirit fills us with a form of His presence so that we are sealed unto Him until the day we meet God in the spirit, face to face. Therefore, you should value your life as a resource for doing God's work. That makes you incredibly precious in God's eyes, and your life should humbly reflect this special privilege.

On her Facebook page, Jessica began receiving bullying posts from a classmate named Chloe. She had befriended the girl because Chloe seemed to have few friends and had asked to be Jessica's Facebook friend. But soon after, Chloe's comments turned to taunts about Jessica's extra fifteen pounds and red hair. Hurt, Jessica pretended to go along with Chloe's hurtful posts and put up emoji smiling faces. Then she became angry and decided to confront Chloe. Lying in bed one night trying to imagine what to say, Jessica realized she did not really want to hurt the girl. Chloe still did not have any friends, and there was nothing Jessica did not like about her – except the spiteful remarks. "Let's have lunch," she responded to Chloe's next nasty comment. Chloe posted a perplexing emoji with a brief "OK." Meeting at the park, the girls brought fast food and at first chatted about school events and upcoming holidays. Then Jessica asked, "Do you really not like me?"

Surprised and embarrassed, Chloe's face turned red, and she sputtered, "I was just teasing you."

Jessica did not think that was true but decided not to pursue it further. She began asking friendly questions about Chloe's family life and found that the girl's parents had divorced a couple years before, and now Chloe went back and forth between her parents, who grilled Chloe on the other parent's whereabouts and actions. She was miserable at being a pawn in her parents' ongoing conflict, and she had no siblings to share the burden. Jessica expressed compassion and suggested they study for the next chemistry quiz, to which Chloe readily agreed. Within a few weeks, the girls became friends, and Chloe's harsh comments on social media stopped. Jessica and Chloe attended the Christmas play at Jessica's church, and Chloe now asks questions about the Bible and promises to think about coming to Sunday service when Jessica invited her.

One of the greatest lessons we learn about love is as follows: love looks past wrongs, and it seeks the good in others. Love always sets a positive example.

As we bring this book to a conclusion by ending in the Book of Titus, which is where we started, we understand that as Christians, we must be in the world but not of the world. We engage with the culture primarily for one reason: to win souls for Christ. That must be done strategically in obedience to God's plan and principles. Our lives must represent Christianity at its best to show honor to God and to inform secular culture that there is a better way to live. Paul summarizes our Christian duties in his letter to Titus:

Remind them to be subject to rulers and authorities, to obey, to be ready for every good work, to speak evil of no one, to be peaceable, gentle, showing all humility to all men. For we ourselves were also once foolish, disobedient, deceived, serving various lusts and pleasures, living in malice and envy, hateful and hating one another. But when the kindness and the love of God our Savior toward man appeared, not by works of righteousness which we have done, but according to His mercy He saved us, through the washing of regeneration and renewing of the Holy Spirit, whom He poured out on us abundantly through Jesus Christ our Savior, that having been justified by His grace we should become heirs according to the hope of eternal life.

(Titus 3:1-7 NKJV)

Encouragement

*The grace of the Lord Jesus Christ, and the love of God,
and the communion of the Holy Spirit be with you all.
Amen.*

(II Corinthians 13:14 NKJV)

Christians remain at spiritual war with secular culture. We are not the only ones doing battle with the popular social, spiritual, and political influences of our time. Secular authors and Christian writers have published books expressing similar concerns, like *A War for the Soul of America, Culture Wars,* and *Jesus and the Culture Wars.* These titles demonstrate public interest in and growing alarm in response to the role of culture in personal and national identity and the future of our society.

The dichotomy that Christians face is to resist the world's influence while demonstrating God's love. We are to acknowledge the appeal of culture while rejecting its power. Culture is everywhere, from the foods we eat to the clothes we wear and the social movements we embrace. Trends in relationships, jobs, raising children, education, money management, and personal style dominate news reports, entertainment options, and social media. We are members of society and observers of culture, but we must carefully pick and choose how we will engage with our worldly environment.

Follow Biblical Examples

In both the Old Testament and the New Testament, God has provided numerous examples of Godly leadership - men and women who trusted God and obeyed his commandments. Abraham, Moses, Ruth, Deborah, and many others whose names appear in Hebrews 11—the Bible's Hall of Fame—set inspiring examples that remain relevant for believers today. We just need to study God's chosen leaders to understand what they did and how they did it. Not everyone can be a Moses, but some of us can follow the example of Joshua, Moses's aide, and a stalwart military commander.

Joshua's commission from the Lord was vast and complex: He was to lead the Israelites that Moses had freed from Egyptian bondage into the Promised Land, given them by God. This meant confronting pagan cultures that detested the Israelites and tried to destroy their entire race. When Jewish spies were sent to spy out the land, they came back with frightening reports: Some regions were inhabited by giants while others were guarded by fierce, highly experienced warriors. Over many years, Joshua led the Israeli army into battles throughout the

Promised Land in keeping with the Lord's commands and provision. Little by little, the territories were won, claimed, and
settled by the twelve tribes of Israel—all thanks to Joshua's
bravery and wisdom in leading God's chosen people to victory:

*Only be strong and very courageous, that you may observe
to do according to all the law which Moses My servant
commanded you; do not turn from it to the right hand or
to the left, that you may prosper wherever you go.*
(Joshua 1:7 NKJV)

If the people obeyed God's laws, they would have His protection. If they did not obey, they would be defeated. This pattern was consistently evidenced when the Israelites listened to
God and were successful, but when they ignored Him, they
failed. King Saul, the first appointed over God's people, is the
particular example of what happens when someone follows his
own inclinations rather than obey God.

Christians in the twenty-first century must also find God-
honoring leaders to follow. Often this will be a church pastor
or minister who preaches the Gospel and consistently obeys
the Bible, leading his congregation by example. Christian mentors, Bible teachers, and older or experienced Godly friends
and family members can also lead believers on the path to sanctification. Sometimes an accountability team or a long-time
church leader can help to guide us on our way.

Build a Strong Relationship with God

If your smartphone runs out of power, you have to recharge it for renewed energy. The same is true for all significant communication devices. If they are disconnected from their power source for long, they become useless. This principle applies to us as Christians. We draw inspiration, strength, and protection from God by staying connected to Him. Bible study, prayer, praise, worship, and fellowship with other believers are the spiritual power sources that keep us energized to do the work that God intends us to carry out. If we get disconnected from God, we will lose our spiritual way, become lost and disoriented, and be of no use in helping others find their way to God.

In today's confusing and demanding culture, it is easy to lose sight of priorities. We mean well and want to keep God first in daily life, but too often, strengthening a relationship with Him slips to the bottom of our to-do list. Satan's number one goal is to keep people away from God. His job becomes easier when unbelievers are attracted to the glittering opportunities of this world instead of connecting to Christian believers and the Bible or a church. Satan and his demonic assistants also likely find it amusing fun to keep Christians spinning in circles instead of purposefully following God's commands in the wake of a spiritual leader.

If we are truthful about it, how many of us reach for the Bible first thing in the morning on the bedside stand instead of a smartphone? How many talk to God before conversing with others? At work, are you more likely to discuss the latest political news or controversial film than what you learned in church last Sunday? How much time do you spend with other believers in ministry or community volunteerism with Christian groups?

Take inventory of a typical day, which for most people includes about sixteen waking hours. What percentage of that time is devoted to fellowshipping with God, studying His Word, and linking with other believers for church outreach or ministry? Are you studying the Bible with your wife or husband? Do you instruct your child according to Biblical principles? How do you treat your neighbors? Of all the people who know you, including acquaintances, how many know you are a Christian? Of these, have any been impacted by their interactions with you?

Jesus taught His disciples and the crowds through his words and his example that daily life could be a distraction. He reminded us through principles and deeds to put God first, as demonstrated in the Lord's Prayer. He also reminded us that if we prioritized our connection to God, our primary needs would be met:

> *But seek first the kingdom of God and His righteousness, and all these things shall be added to you.*
> (Matthew 6:33 NKJV)

Learning from others how to live as a Christian and making God a daily priority lays the foundation for living a holy life that can influence others' salvation. The culture will always be around us and trying to stifle or even destroy the Christian faith. As we learn from the examples of others how a Christian should behave and establish an unbreakable connection with God for the power of the Holy Spirit to work through us, one more thing we should strive for is to let God's love shine through us.

SHINE GOD'S LOVE

It is believed that Nellie Talbot wrote the lyrics of a popular children's church hymn called "I'll Be a Sunbeam," which was set to music by Edwin O. Excell in 1900. This is the first stanza:

Jesus wants me for a sunbeam,
To shine for Him each day;
In every way, try to please Him,
At home, at school, at play.

This well-known song has been sung by generations of children to celebrate the joy of living for Jesus. Although simple in meaning and melody, the words remind us of the privilege it is to serve God in all of our daily activities. Reminding ourselves of these innocent lyrics may help to maintain our spiritual focus.

Often, Christians get caught up in the anxieties and distress of this world. We become distracted from our real purpose, which is to honor God and reflect His love in everything we do. No one is perfect, of course, and we all fail at times. But we can make this simple task our central goal in going about each day's activities.

Have you ever met someone who seemed happy and contented for no particular reason? Joy might seem to emanate from their face, and an unexplainable light shines from their eyes. Often, you find out that individual is a Christian. Their faith cannot be hidden, and their joy is contagious. God is pleased by our radiance as we realize and celebrate our unique standing and destiny as God's chosen children.

But let all those rejoice who put their trust in You; let them ever shout for joy, because You defend them; let those also who love Your name Be joyful in You.
(Psalms 5:11 (NKJV)

Sometimes in this troubled world, we forget who created us, why we are here, and where we are going. Instead, we get bogged down in the misery of a moment, forgetting that God is our ever-present help in times of trouble. When the world sees us in the condition of defeat, people wonder, "Why should I become a Christian? They are no happier than I am despite their so-called faith and forgiveness."

Just knowing God should be cause enough for rejoicing! To have a relationship with Him is beyond incredible, and to have the promise of an eternal future in his presence is the pinnacle of joy. Each day, remind yourself of who God is, what He has done, and where you are headed. If that does not bring a smile to your face, something is seriously wrong!

Twenty-one-year-old Terrence walked around his housing complex, picking up trash, whistling a tune that most who heard did not recognize, as they were not church attendees. He helped an elderly woman get out of a cab and carried her groceries to the door of her garden apartment. When she offered to pay him, he smiled broadly and protested, "No ma'am, I'm happy to help. I did it for you *and* the Lord."

Surprised, the white-haired lady smiled faintly. "I remember hearing that song the last time I went to church," she said. "But I can hardly get out now with my back pain."

Terrence grinned and told her the radio station where his church broadcast every Sunday at 11 a.m. He also mentioned another church with a similar denomination that was on local TV on Sunday mornings.

"Thank you, young man." She smiled again, and with a wave, disappeared through her door as Terrence waved back and continued working his way through the grounds to pick up litter left by careless residents.

Whatever our circumstances, whoever we meet even briefly, we must remember that God has orchestrated every event to provide an opportunity to point others to Him. Love for God and for others should guide our actions. Each morning, we can pray to ask God to move us in the direction He wants us to go for that day.

In these times, trouble abounds. The wicked are becoming braver. Godly people are being persecuted. The culture in which we live is like a boiling cauldron teeming with filth and evil of all kinds. We must avoid immersion in it at all costs. But we also must represent God's love to those who need it most, as the Apostle Paul reminds us:

> *And though I have the gift of prophecy, and understand all mysteries and all knowledge, and though I have all faith, so that I could remove mountains, but have not love, I am nothing.*
>
> (I Corinthians 13:2 NKJV)

Walk circumspectly and be careful of the company you keep unless it is for witnessing purposes. Seek God's face each day and His forgiveness at night.

> *He has shown you, O man, what is good; and what does the Lord require of you but to do justly, to love mercy, and to walk humbly with your God?*
>
> (Micah 6:8 NKJV)

EPILOG

If we are to maintain a sense of purpose, we must remain faithful to the Word of God. This book challenges the believer to walk a path that is totally different from the world. We are to be the lights of the world and the salt of the earth. It is my prayer that you enjoy your Christian journey and, in all things, give thanks to God. Remember, He has promised to keep us in perfect peace as we keep our mind stayed on Him.

Grace and Peace to all!

CPSIA information can be obtained
at www.ICGtesting.com
Printed in the USA
BVHW081931270521
608336BV00003B/6